Million Dollar Ferrari Sports Cars to Beat-Up Old Ford Trucks, Classic Mopar Hot Rods to Innovative Chevy Rat Rods, Vintage Trans Am Racing to Cars and Coffee Meetings

Classic Car Stories

By Isaiah Cox

Table of Contents

What's the Deal With Vintage Racing?

You ever wonder what is the deal with those guys that run old slow cars around the track at "vintage races" when there's so many modern, quick options? I mean, a Miata smokes almost every one of those old sport cars, right? Why would you ever waste money running something old and slow? At the last Portland Historic Races it struck me how few people were in the stands, our culture has no understanding of how exciting these vintage sports cars are, as well as the times and history they represent.

I've thrown this together as a primer. If I can share with you some of the stories I (think I) know, you might gain a fresh appreciation for vintage sport car racing. And if you're one of my friends, maybe you won't think I'm so weird for spending time and money on my 1957 sports car when your Accord is faster!

For your sake I'm going to greatly abridge this and only hit you with some mountain-top highs of the sport. Due to the litigious nature of our society I'm going to have to use photos I've captured rather than more applicable period photos easily available on the internet because someone will threaten to sue me (it's already happened on my free blog). So not every picture will match the topic exactly, but I did the best I can with my photo stock. Remember Peter Egan's seminal work on car short stories, *Side Glances*, didn't have any photos!

I might get a few things wrong or slightly off because until someone pays me to do this I just don't have time to research and write a novel titled "The History of Racing". Someone else has anyways. And it's awesome. If you only have 20 minutes, read this. Or if you have 5 hours to invest, you should watch the Shell series The

History of Racing available on YouTube (https://www.youtube.com/watch?v=OROeC3_Zt78&list=PLEEC587278736BB88).

If you don't have time for Shell, well then read on.

What's considered the first car race occurred in 1894 in France. Many of the cars were steered by a rudder type setup. The 1st across the line was a gentleman named de Dion but he was disqualified because his car was more of a train, running on steam using a stoker system. Second across the line was a Peugeot. This might be the last race that a Peugeot won. Somewhat fitting for a car made in France, who have not won a war of their own accord since the 1800s.

I'm kidding, Peugeot made some great racing cars during these early years and even won the Indy 500 state side.

De Dion is a well known name in car circles because shortly thereafter he designed a rear axle that allowed each wheel to move up and down independently. It was largely ignored and cars typically had one piece rear axles. 60 Years later Jaguar adapted this De Dion rear end into their E Type sports car. Since then all sports cars have went that direction in some form, the last holdout being the Ford Mustang, who in 2015 finally adopted an independent rear end... 115 years after Mr. de Dion invented it. Way to adapt quickly Ford!

France continued to be the leader in car racing. England instituted some weird laws due to public concern about car/horse interactions. You could have a car, but you had to hire someone to walk in front of you with a flag. No wonder Mr. Toad craved speed, he was stifled by British law!

Scarcely 9 years later cars had come a long way. Instead of rudders, some cars had steering wheels, and the overall shape was beginning to resemble less a "horseless carriage" and more our traditional car.

Unfortunately safety had not progressed along with the car. Tires were still solid, suspension almost non-existent, brakes minimal, center-of-gravity high, etc. The Paris-Madrid race of 1903 was actually France's last open-road race. In the passenger/mechanic seat of the car leading the race was one of the Renault brothers. After the first day of racing French government stepped in and stopped the race after nine fatalities, including the brother of Mr. Renault who was following behind in another race car.

On the American side of the pond, oval racing became popular. This author's opinion is that this may have stemmed from the velodromes that were common to bicycle racing prior to the autos proliferation. As oval racing is a far cry from open-road, sport car racing, other than this mention this blog will stay away from the rich history of oval racing.

Eddie Rickenbacker was one of the famous pre-WW1 American racing heroes. His autobiography is a must have. His father died when he was 8. Eddie went to work at a local factory to help support his family (he was the oldest child). While working at the factory he took by-mail engineering courses. His engineering background gave him an opportunity to work at an auto-shop. The shop sponsored race cars and Eddie was given the opportunity to drive. He became an American racing hero due to his success, nicknamed "Fast Eddie".

At the outbreak of WW1, Eddie was technically too old to become a pilot. So he travelled to France and showed up at the base of the Hat-in-the-Ring flying squadron. In an odd coincident, he had previously helped the base commander fix his car back in the states. The base commander let Rickenbacker learn to fly.

By the end of the war Eddie was America's leading Ace and the leader of the Hat-in-the-Ring squadron.

Eddie went on to own the Indianapolis Speedway, and Eastern Air Lines. In addition, he was a WW2 spy to Russia because Russia wanted his advice on their planes. Rickenbacker crashed at sea in a B-17, surviving with his crew on a floating raft for close to a month. A Christian, he had a small bible in his suit and Eddie instituted daily bible studies on the raft. The experience brought several of his co-raftees to belief.

His autobiography includes some prototype testing he was involved with, including a photo of a rocket powered backpack the pilot would wear. Eddie's life reads like a science-fiction, adventure novel. Then you read who endorses the book. Jimmy Doolittle and a President. No fiction here. Fast Eddie was a model American, through and through. Anyways, I've digressed a lot, but Rickenbacker's autobiography was one of the best books I've ever read and I take every opportunity to tell people about it.

Back to racing.

In 1907 England opened the 1st purpose built racetrack, Brooklands. Built with steep banking, the intent was that cars that drove near the top would need to turn little or at all on the banking. The track was fast but bumpy. The sectional concrete paving technique was the cause of the bumpy ride. Brooklands stayed a track until WW2, although as speed increased it wasn't uncommon for Brooklands to send cars airborne.

During WW2 Brooklands was used for an airstrip and parts of the track were destroyed during bombing raids, or taken out for facilities.

James May, of Top Gear fame, recreated the Brooklands track using the local community and Scalextric race cars and track. It's a fun watch (http://www.hulu.com/watch/323938).

WW1 put a pause to motor racing. The world was involved in one of it's most deadly and brutal struggles. 16 million men died, and 20 million were injured.

After WW1 the world slowly recovered and again men set their mind to finding ways to appease their desire for adventure.

It's important to keep in mind, these cars were far from docile. They had large iron motors that propelled the cars along at great speeds, but seldom had brakes to match the power of their momentum. In addition, there were little to no safety considerations. Videos of Brooklands racing are ripe with people flying off the top of the track. There was no seat belt or roll bar, so the drivers best hope was to be thrown clear of the machine. The tiny windscreens provided little protection and it was common for drivers to have rocks and birds hit them in the face at 100+ mph, including one of the Le Mans winning Bentley drivers (who, coincidentally, had been refreshing himself with Cognac during pit stops).

It was at this time Bentley established their reputation.

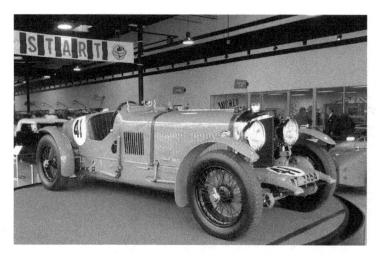

From 1924 to 1930 Bentleys won 5 of the Le Mans races, an epic 24 hour race on a road circuit in France. Obviously the course was closed but some of the locals refused to recognize the closure of the road for the race. One of the old ladies that lived along the route was famous for walking across the track in indifference to the race in order to visit with her neighbors.

Almost equally as dominating as the Bentleys at Le Mans was the Type 35 Bugatti in the World Championship races. Statistically the Type 35 has over 1000 registered wins. It was a dominating Grand Prix race car and in 1926 took the world championship.

Another period contender for top dog was Alfa Romeo. In 1925 Alf Romeo introduced their straight 8 motor and won the first ever world championship series. One of Alfa's top aces was the celebtrated racer Nuvolari.

This straight 8 Alfa design continued on through the early 30s. Alfa vied with Bugatti, Delage (French), Mercedes, and Bentley for racing supremacy.

National pride was endowed to each of these manufacturers. The whole country followed the races to

see if their countries car would win the world
championship.

It was at this time that a former racer, Enzo Ferrari, took
on management of the Alfa Romeo team. A WW1
veteran, he was approached by the family of a famous
WW1 Italian ace who requested that their sons family
crest be applied to the Italian Alfa racing cars as a good
luck symbol easily identifiable to Italians. Ferrari agreed
and thus was established possibly the most famous
automotive symbol, the prancing horse later to be used
as Ferrari's emblem. Not many people know that the
Alfa Romeo team originally wore the prancing horse.

In 1933 Adolf Hitler and the Nazi party came to power in
Germany. The Nazi's were set on making the other
nations recognize their supremacy in all things,
including motor racing. The Nazis funneled money into

race car development and the Mercedes race cars leaped ahead in technological innovation. The W25 Mercedes replaced Mercedes outdated SSK (designed by one Ferdinand Porsche). The motor in the W25 would eventually reach near 500 hp.

Now the Mercedes and the Audis of this period can barely be considered sports cars, but the Alfas, Bentleys and Bugattis they were racing against are seen on the road to this day, so by default we'll lump them in with sports cars. In truth though, these were probably the first cars that could be considered pure race car.

It was at this time that the previously mentioned Nuvolari made what may be the greatest victory of all time.

The Nazi party had been pouring money into the Mercedes and Audi teams (we'll discuss Audi in a minute). They also poured money into their tracks.

In 1935, at Germany's famous Nurbergring, in front of the leading members of the Nazi party, driving an outdated Alfa Romeo, Nuvolari defeated the German cars and took the checkered flag. Beyond being an unbelievable drive, it was a slap in the face for the domineering, brooding, fearsome Nazi party. This may be one of the greatest under-dog car racing stories of all time.

We haven't talked about the fearsome Auto Union Type D yet, but it deserves equal mention. It's said that few men could drive this rear engined monstrosity. The Auto Union and the Mercedes were dubbed the "silver arrows".

Hans Stuck was the most notable Type D driver. His epic charge of the Austrian Glossglockner is still talked about, Classic and Sports Car magazine recently taking an Auto Union Type D out to the mountain to recreate the experience. So successful was Stuck and the Type D at hill climbs, Stuck was nicknamed, "the king of the mountains" in German. Stuck's last hill climb championship was at age 60 when he was the German hill climb champion.

The Germans touted their race cars as a matter of Nazi pride.

In 1937 the Germans improved their track at Avus with an extremely banked corner so their cars could maintain speed through the corner demonstrating how fast they truly were at nearly 500 hp.

Because Avis wasn't on the World Championship circuit, streamlined bodies were allowed. Mercedes and Auto Union created two of the most beautiful pre-war cars ever made for this race, but on top of their smooth lines & shiny metal bodies their nazi emblems dripped with an ominous current.

But half a world away, another star was coming into his own. The year was 1938 and Juan Fangio started racing in Argentina with a beat up Ford V8. Fangio was 28. By 1940, in a Chevy, Fangio had become Argentina's champion.

After the war Fangio began racing in Europe. He won, and won, and won. His nickname became "El Maestro". He won 5 world championships, the last in 1957 at the age of 47 years old. He retired in 1958. He won 24 of the 52 formula one races he participated in.

Fangio went to whatever team he thought he'd have the most success with. In the 1950s he bounced around Alfa Romeo, Mercedes, Ferrari and Maserati.

If you'd like to see the Maestro at work, there's a great video on Youtube of the 1955 Belgium Grand Prix in which he destroys his competitors (https://www.youtube.com/watch?v=7exBtOgys7I). It isn't even a race.

Days after the Belgian Grand Prix, the worst tragedy in all of racing history occurred, and Fangio drove through it. At Le Mans a pitting car forced another car to swerve around it. The Mercedes car following the swerving car hit the rear fender and was directed airborne into the crowd. 83 spectators, and the driver were killed. At the end of the 1955 world championship, Mercedes withdrew from racing until the 1980s.

I wish the 1955 Le Mans were a happier note, as my car made it's racing debut there.

If you watch the 1955 Belgium race you'll note that Fangio's teammate, Stirling Moss, also dominates the rest of the pack finishing close behind Fangio. That same year Moss beat the Italians on their own roads at the most famous road race still in existance, the Mille Miglia (Thousand Miles). Moss' performance, both in Grand Prix and road racing/rallying, led many to believe he would be the next great. Unfortunately a terrible accident in 1961 ended his career. He continues to this day to be a great advocate of vintage car racing. The British have knighted him and regard him as a national hero.

In a video on Youtube, the famous actor Patrick Steward takes lessons from Moss in an effort to emulate him (https://www.youtube.com/watch?v=UtRWhPQVAY8). It's a great watch.

Across the pond, over here in America, the introduction of the Corvette and T-bird had ignited a road racing passion. Road racing became trendy with the youth and road races were packed with young men wanting to try their machines, and the stands were filled with the girls and families that had come to watch. Adding also to the passion were the WW2 veterans, who had seen the european sport cars during their deployment and desired them.

One of the most famous of these racers was one Carroll Shelby. A (failed) chicken farmer from Texas, he became a diplomat to the European racing circuits when his fast racing won him a seat on the World Championship circuit. Carroll wanted to stay true to his roots and he'd often wear overalls and a cowboy hat at the races.

In 1959 Carroll and a teammate won Le Mans. It was the first time an American had ever won Le Mans.

A heart condition caused Mr Shelby to retire after the Le Mans victory but he would be back in a prominent way in the history of road racing.

Also of note, one of the most successful women drivers appeared on the scene in the late 50's, and she was the sister of none other than Stirling Moss.

A replica of Pat Moss' car

Pat Moss out and out beat everyone (men included) in the 1960 Leige-Rome-Leige rally. Moss continued to be a prominent player in rally racing well into the 60s, including an important early win for the mini Cooper at the 1962 Tulip Rally.

The Mini Cooper. Specifically in "S" spec, challenged everything anyone believed. It's light weight, peppy motor, affordable cost, low center of gravity, incredible handling and ease to maintain led to many successes over much bigger, faster cars. It won the Monte Carlo rally outright three times. The Mini Cooper S was nicknamed "the Giant Killer".

Remember old Carroll Shelby? Well, around this time he got it in his head that what the world needed was a car with European handling but American muscle. Many of the British sport cars had little 4 or 6 cylinders, while the Corvettes touted V8s.

Shelby talked Ford into providing motors, and AC into providing a chasis, for an American powered sports car.

The Shelby Cobra was born.

Well, back when Carroll had been racing, Ferrari had extended a factory racing seat and when Carroll arrived in Italy, old man Ferrari reneged. Carroll now had a burning passion to beat Ferrari at sports car racing. Plus, Carroll's blood pumped American. He wanted to see an American sports car win the world championship.

On the short courses his Cobra's blew the Ferrari's out of the water (once he'd figured out how to keep the axles together, the ACs not being up to the task). But unfortunately on the long tracks, the Cobra suffered from an aerodynamic problem; the Cobra wasn't aerodynamic.

Carroll and his team went to work on an aerodynamic coupe version of the Cobra. The Shelby Daytona was born. The Daytona won the World Championship in 1965, beating Ferrari.

Shelby then went to work with Ford on the GT40, which defeated Ferrari's 6 year winning streak at Le Mans in 1966.

Back on our side of the pond, Ford's partnership with Shelby led to some fast Mustangs produced with Shelby racing generated technology. The Camaro was pressed to keep up.

The Trans Am racing series pitted the two against each other. Whoever posted wins on Sunday meant sales at the dealership on Monday.

Roger Penske, a famous ex-racer, partnered with Chevy to run the Camaro team. In 1967 the fledgling Camaro didn't show much promise, but Penske felt certain he could sort the car out.

And they famously cheated.

Chevy pressed thin steel for the '67 race car. When weighed after it's only 67 win, it was found to be 250 pounds lighter than the minimum weight. Trans Am only allowed the win to stay in place because Penske threatened that Chevy would back out of the Trans Am series. They did ban the car from racing in future years.

For 1968 Penske acid dipped his cars. Then added the weight back in at key places that would keep the center of gravity low and aid handling. There's a story of someone leaning against the roof and causing a hand print in the thin metal.

Also, Penske again snuck the 1967 lightweight car in to races. They switched out the grille and other items for a 1968. Then they had a different 1968 car pass tech inspection. After the 68 passed they'd slap the stickers on the 67 and race the banned 1967 lightweight car.

 The Penske team won 10 of 13 races in 1968, winning the Trans Am title. They repeated the feat in 1969, again winning the title.

After Trans Am, I can't think of any significant sports car racing. Sure, there's been more Le Mans races. And the Sports Car Club of America keeps on holding events. But there's no racing series with street drive-able sports cars that captivates the world with it's results. Race results don't make or break a car makers sales. Nations don't anxiously follow race results.

Those old cars you see going around the track at vintage races stand for so much more than car racing. National pride was at play when they raced. The men that raced them were giants of men, heroes to their nation and in some cases, the world. Nations watched those old cars race in awe. Auto makers watched the races knowing that the race results would make them or break them. Names like Bentley, Ferrari and Shelby were established by the results those old cars posted.

Modern cars can go around the track faster (in most cases) but the modern cars don't have the rich heritage of vintage race cars. That's why I choose to pursue vintage racing. In some way I want to associate with the rich history of these old cars. I want to see Nuvolari's car and imagine the Nazi's staring at it in hate. I want to see Fangio's car and imagine El Maestro. I want to race my MGA and imagine what a 1955 Le Mans (before the accident) must have been like. I'd like to build a Daytona replica and see just what it was that Shelby came up with for America.

It's vintage racing for me.

S.O.B. Racing - Budget Vintage Racing

If several like-minded individuals were to join my racing endeavors we would name our team S.O.B. Racing, for Scrape-On-By Racing. An appropriate name for three reasons: 1. financially the team could only scrape together funds to pay for racing and vehicle prep, 2. the old heaps we choose to race may scrape back to the pits after breaking, and 3. if you consider other words S.O.B. might stand for, it would reflect the words used when our vehicles failed inspection or scraped back to the pit.

In a world where vintage racing is considered cool, and events like the Goodwood Revival are drawing thousands of fans, S.O.B. Racing would be the quid-essential vintage racing team. Now that made men, near retirement and enjoying the fruits of their labor can afford to tune their E-Type Jaguar to a degree of reliability that never existed in the 60s, S.O.B. Racing would be the only team still in their 20s battling un-enhanced MGB technology, as was done in the 1960s.

I own the MGB, un-restored and un-glorious in its lack of technology. The car is equipped with leaky lever action shocks, an alternator that won't run the motor/ heater/windshield wipers at the same time, fans that seize in a shrill scream, and worn out rubber bushings that make noises when exiting corners that make a driver fear that in the next corner the steering mechanism may or may not make the expected turn of the wheels.

Don't get me wrong, I'm happy to own the MGB. What other vehicle could I approach a track in for the price of a Ford Taurus (my only asset which I sold to buy my MGB)?

On race day, the B and its 1960's technology are in stark contrast to the Corvettes, BMW Mini-Coopers and Miatas. At the last auto-cross day I had to react quickly to three issues with the MGB while the other drivers were only concerned whether their tires were holding the right air pressure (little knowing that for $500 dollars more than their tires cost they too could have purchased my car… actually, they probably all knew).

After several weeks of preparing the car (thicker oil in the shocks, greasing all the zerts, cleaning the oil off the motor and transmission, welding up the holes in the exhaust and floorboard, pulling the trim off the wheels, checking all the fluid levels, and removing the hardtop) I thought I was ready. I approached the race expecting to breeze through inspection.

The B almost failed inspection; it turned out the new plastic (because that's all they sell) battery strap had snapped, probably during the last autocross. After much begging and pleading, tech let me pass with a crisscrossing of zip ties (don't leave home without them) and a strong advisory that I would not pass my next tech inspection unless it was properly strapped.

After my first lap of the course I saw people running towards my car which is never a good thing. Fearing fire I was relieved to find out the new Le Mans style flip-up gas cap was not sealed and every time I turned left hard a stream of gas appeared out the rear of the car. Again, much begging took place and they eventually let me continue with a t-shirt jammed in the tank tube to stop the gas from coming out.

Then, while waiting in line for another lap, I was again approached by a now grim official. The B was leaking antifreeze from the radiator overflow. I learned why old racers would put beer cans at the bottom of their overflow tube. Misting the radiator with water solved the problem but again, I was almost eliminated and much begging took place.

All the while the modern cars took lap after lap of the course with no problems at all, missing the experience of vintage racing. S.O.B. Racing understands what it means to be vintage cool; you must have dirty hands, quick thinking and the ability to plead with course officials to truly be retro. I'll fix the problems I know about for the next race (already made a cool aluminum battery strap) and come mentally prepared to react quickly... and beg.

Video Link:

http://www.youtube.com/watch?v=_L1nyCqWpRc

Portland Swap Meet... wait no... PIR Auto Swap

A buddy called me up and asked if I wanted to go the Portland Swap Meet. Billed as the largest swap meet on the West Coast I was looking forward to it. I'm not sure why though, I've been in the past and the best things I can remember pulling out were a sarcastic poster (now posted in my garage) and a vintage racing sticker. But the hope was there that I'd stumble upon something I need, like $50 MGA fenders without rust holes.

We got off the interstate at Portland International Raceway (PIR) because I'd remembered there was swap meet activity at PIR as well as the Expo Center and PIR was closer to us. Only when writing this blog did I find out that the PIR activity is not actually the Portland Swap Meet but a second event called PIR Auto Swap. So it turns out, I never went to the Portland Swap Meet.

So let's talk about PIR Auto Swap.

Despite the rainy weather there still seemed to be a good crowd. Oddly, though midday Saturday vendors were packing up and going home. Apparently the PIR Auto Swap only goes through Saturday, which seems odd because it doesn't encourage guys that work regular work days to attend. The question the schedule begs to ask is, do people take Friday off for this? Based on what I saw, I wouldn't.

Both my buddy and I left feeling strangely depressed.
Let me try and show you why with pictures.

First the rat rod craze has encouraged every person with
a rusty piece of metal laying a field to slap expensive
price tags on their piles of rust. It's counter-intuitive to
the rat rod movement. The whole reason people
started building rat rods was to escape the disgusting
prices on all the established hot rod parts. Now rat rods
are trendy and pricey. Rat rods gaining in value are a
great example of how the hot rod culture is killing itself
by taking the fun out. The cycle seems to be: start with
something fun, then jack the prices up on everything
and try and make a business out of it, then be unwilling
to come back down on price even though the youth are
losing all interest.

Here are several prime examples of cars so rough that
they should be nearly given to anyone willing to take
them on -

When I was a kid someone gave me a Henry J Kaiser (yes, it looks like a name but it's an old car) for $35. I was so excited. I think we should try that a little more. Maybe we won't get the cash we want, but we'll see some joy in someone else's eye. There's a different value there! Our culture needs more of that. I'm probably guilty as well, but in my defense I did just give some cheap KC style headlights to the neighbor kid. Not a car though.

Back to the swap meet.

Beyond rusty car hulks, there was junk everywhere! Not just car junk, but any sort of junk you can think of. People have watched too many episodes of American Restoration/Pickers and think that everything fifteen years or older should be worth something (and often they think boo-koo bucks).

$650 for this old bike. Yeah, maybe it's neat, but not $650 neat!!!

And how 'bout a Dr. Suess clock?

In many stalls stuff was piled so deep you just couldn't take it all in. You found yourself just skimming because you couldn't afford the mental strain to register all the little things being sold. You might have more interest if you thought you were going to find a deal, but when you did see something you might want it was often higher than retail. For example, MGA disc brake pads, - $100. You can buy the highest grade for $45 from Moss Motors. I mentioned this to the retailer and all she did was glare at me.

Or how about a plastic kayak for $500? How much could a plastic kayak possibly be new?! Oh, and paddle is extra.

Broken, cracked fiberglass hull of an ugly motorcycle sidecar - $100

Now to be fair, I've always wondered where to find two foot tall ghetto rims. Turns out, at the swap meet. Only $1650! Brand new chromed wire wheels for my 1957 car cost $1600 as a reference.

Another thing I saw was a remarkable number of broke down looking motors with stickers talking about how they were almost new. I saw, "just rebuilt", "new pistons and rings", etc. Right. That's why you're selling them. Because they worked so well.

Now you may think, "Well, he's just taking pictures of the worst things he saw."

Nope, I just took pictures when I remembered to pull the camera out. It got to be a game between my friend and I. We'd see something and then we'd name ridiculous prices as we approached it seeing who was closer.

I remember one in detail. A broke down go-kart with a plastic 4x4 body.

Me - "They're going to want something ridiculous like $800"

Andrew - "No way. $600"

The sticker - $1100

This process repeated itself many times.

And why do all the old Dodges get pulled apart? I saw more Mopar parts than you could spit at (seriously, you'd be dry mouthed long before the last). And who is paying $1800 for the intake setup? I'm sure someone. In the picture below it's a Chrysler 300 intake in the middle (yes, it's ford on the left, but there was less of that; except Mustang parts were EVERYWHERE).

I overheard one guy ask the seller why his old chainsaws were so expensive. The seller responded, "Well, they're man wall art now!"

But at least there were video games. Anyone else find it ironic being on a track pretending to drive a race car, and then wandering around it looking at old junk that was once used to make cars fast? Could be a statement about where our culture has went but I'll try to let it go....

Now in all fairness I did see things I would like to own or could at least appreciate.

The Camaro had already sold so I'm not sure the price but I do like the paint job and hide-a-way headlights.

This teeny trailer was fun looking. It was about the size of a small tent. I guess it would be great for those who hate tent poles.

These VW pull wagons were the most creative things I saw all day. Loved them.

This Mopar looked like it could make a beefy project for $750. Unfortunately, based on all the parts I saw in other booths I'd be willing to bet there wasn't a thing left under the hood.

This land cruiser looked like it could have a lot of fun potential. Unfortunately I also noticed (and you can see in the pics) the front brake lines are clamped off by a vice grip. Not a good sign.

And for some odd reason I love big straight motors. Unfortunately I think they wanted some insane price like $14,000 for this chassis.

But about the time we had given up on finding anything that seemed of value we happened across this bug which ran and seemed pretty clean inside for $1500.

Someone could find a fun low cost project car here! The options were limited though.

No cost on a circle track car, nor a lurking seller. Looks like it would be a blast.

A little French car would be tempting for $500. They wanted $8k. The only little French car project I'd pay $8k for is one of those old airplane motor propeller powered jobs from the early 1900s.

It was fun to see an original interior in an old Chevy. It was more ornate than I expected. I think a lot of people don't put the full interior in when they restore them so you're used to seeing customs that are light on interior from this time period.

Another weird thing, in a way the people seemed sad. Literally sad, mopey, downtrodden, etc. When Andrew purchased a tow rope shackle thing, he told the owner "this is the first thing I've bought today".

The man replied, "Well, you better spend some money! People need to eat man!"

It seemed as though many of these sellers truly believed their things were worth what they were asking for. And instead of letting the market dictate the price, they seemed to look at us as disrespectful because we weren't willing to pay what they thought the things are worth.

As we left, tired and dejected from not finding anything fun (I bought a weed-eater), we saw this car being pulled out of the mud in the parking lot. Somehow it seemed a fitting note to end our day at the track swap meet we both agreed.

But we were far from done yet. The flaggers sent us out an exit route that avoided direct exit to the interstate and instead sent us on a 20 minute jaunt into the commercial district on the banks of the back waters of the Willamette where the police will occasionally find bodies.

I hope the real swap meet was more fun with better, more exciting finds. Next year I bet I'll try the one at the Expo Center, the real Portland Swap Meet, hopeful as ever. It's amazing what a year or two will do to your memory.

1st Week With An MGA

I watched two years of progress drive away two weeks ago in order to fund my new project, a 1958 MGA coupe. It was strangely sad, I never expected watching my 1979 MGB drive away would elicit much emotion, let alone strong emotion, but there I was chasing the buyer down the parking lot to tell him yet another little idiosyncrasy. It was partly because I couldn't bear to see it drive away, and partly because I feared that if I didn't tell him every little thing he'd fire bomb my front porch someday based on non-disclosure of all issues; a salesman I am not. Frankly, I'm surprised he still bought it.

I'd found an MGA on Craigslist that I could afford. In other words, it didn't run and was starting to rot away. But it was in much better shape than the last MGA I'd considered trading the MGB for, which had been laying in a field with the hood open and the head off the motor.

I don't know why but I'm obsessed with the MGA body style but I believe the MGA to be one of the best-looking cars ever made. The price was a little steep for my MGB sales budget but the owner was willing to come down a little when I assured him it'd be going to a loving home.

A buddy and I picked the car up in Washington last weekend. It felt as though it was meant to be when I had friends volunteer both a truck and trailer and then when hooking them together all the lights worked without changing any wiring! I've never had a truck and trailer come together without a lengthy process of troubleshooting... it was almost eerie. We had an uneventful trip and the transaction went smoothly, the car was just as described and there were no surprises, also rare for Craigslist.

The car is now happily elevated on jack stands in my garage. The first couple days I spent hours sitting in a chair in front of the car staring at it when I wasn't exploring it. I was concerned I'd have buyer's remorse after selling a working, fun MGB for a rusting hulk of an MGA but it was just the opposite. The more I looked at the MGA the happier I was that I'd found it.

I discovered that the car was near complete and original. No one had even cut into the Lucas wiring as it's still wearing it's original fabric sheathing. I found the wiring discovery shocking as it could only mean one of two things: either the car was a complete fluke in that the Lucas electrics worked reliably (one in a million) or the gentleman that drove it was content with not driving at night, or listening to the radio, while using the wipers with discretion in a downpour in an effort to not deplete the battery which had to be recharged after every trip downtown.

Other fun discoveries in the car included: the headliner didn't have a tear in it. The door wore a Texaco sticker from antiquity that recorded its service record, the dash didn't have a tear in the vinyl cover, and the seats were a little dirty but issue free.

As a sports car, the car couldn't be more functional. Behind the grill two fresh air hoses run back to the engine compartment. The motor is fed by twin side-draft carbs, one carb for two cylinders. There are cowl vents for fresh air to the motor. The hood, trunk lid and door skins are made out of aluminum. The seats sit well inside the frame rails to drop the driver down to close to the deck. The car's styling is aerodynamic and born from a time period of Austin-Healey's and AC Aces; the shared heritage shows in the Healey-esque snout and Cobra-esque rear haunches. And who doesn't love banjo steering wheels?

Because the MGA cost slightly more than the MGB, I'm on an imposed budget until next month, which will promote marital health. Based on this limitation I thought I'd tackle something easy and cheap, replacing the plywood floorboards under the seats. Although they looked good I had this nagging thought in the back of my mind "what if you hit a road bump and Kellie (my wife) suddenly disappeared?" Because the marital relations are still good, I thought replacement floorboards were in order.

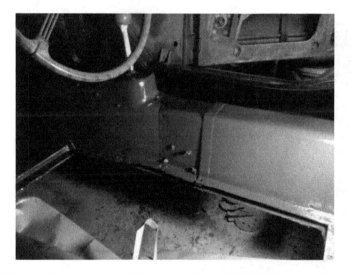

What I thought would be a 3-4 hour project turned into a 12-hour project. Projects sound so simple before you take them on. For example, "replace the floorboards" sounds quite easy but what it really means is, "cut out the old floorboards, take each bolt out individually with vice grips because the screw heads are impossible to turn, sand off as much rust as possible, cut forms out of cardboard, make three trips to the hardware store because you keep forgetting things/getting the wrong things, cut the plywood, drill the bolt holes, stain the wood, mask off the interior that's not floor, urethane the plywood, paint the interior frame and plywood you're leaving in, wait a night, re-drill holes in the correct position, make another trip to home depot for washers and caulk, finish install and finally clean-up".

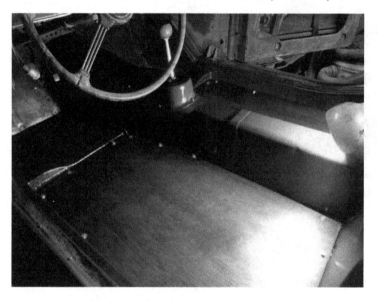

Hopefully Kellie knows I love her... or I would have just done my side. If I was to do it again I might just do her side; my safety has always been less of a priority and my father made the point 1950's plywood probably had better non-water soluble glues anyway.

But I'm on my way, and looking at the base picture of an MGA frame without bodywork, the area I cleaned up was essentially as close to the frame as I could get without doing a frame-up restoration. Unfortunately, although this might be the right car for frame-up restoration, but my tiny apartment garage does not bode well for the concept and I think I'll have to make do without (maybe I'll do the MGA frame up in 20 years when I'm more financially stable and living arrangements are more accommodating). The F-pillars holding the doors are shot so I'll have to replace those, which will be challenging, but the coupe body I think will be able to st

Next month, when I'm allowed a budget again, I think I'll start working on the concept of getting it running. One of the wheels shows evidence of the hub being halfway taken apart so I'm hoping that's what parked the car and the little 1500 cc four cylinder is still capable of moving the car. This seems likely as the odometer reads 10,000 miles and the indications are that this was a reading of 110,000. My old MGB was running fairly strong at 140,000 with a similar motor. I'll likely be writing in a month how this was all wishful thinking, but for now I have hope; it's always more enjoyable to have hope or I'd be depressed about a lot of tasks that could turn into total headaches (rust mitigation, bodywork, paint, motor, transmission, hydraulic systems, brakes, etc.... sigh).

Driving back from the coast the other day I was playing my typical game of spot the neat car in the barn (while Kellie requests that I watch the road) when I realized I now own the car that I would be overjoyed to find in a barn. I still sit in front of it now and stare at it under the guise that I'm talking on the phone so Kellie doesn't think I'm completely nuts. It's just so cool, and I'm really looking forward to the day I can drive it down the road.

Thoughts on Jerome AZ, Hillclimb Racing & Changing Culture

My wife and I recently spent a day in the AZ hill town (also one-time ghost town) of Jerome Arizona. Throughout Jerome, I found evidence of a significant motorcycle and car history. Viewing a large time gap between Jerome's heyday and now, some serious cultural changes were also apparent.

To those of you unfamiliar with Jerome, in the early 20th century Jerome was a thriving mining town, that dwindled with changing copper economies and eventually the mines closed up shop in the 50's. Following the mines closing, the town was largely abandoned until a collection of free thinkers and free rangers seized upon the opportunity for free housing. Eventually, the free thinking collection of inhabitants landed upon thinking of capitalism, and the town populated with artist shops, which now thrive.

As you explore Jerome today you will find several museums and, due to the historic nature of the city, the majority of the remainder of the city can be considered something of a living museum.

Our first stop was the Douglas Mansion. Around 1900 a second main ore body for copper was found in the Jerome hill and an additional claim/mining operation sprung up largely owned and managed by James Douglas. Later in the century, after the closing of the mine, the Douglas mansion was donated to the state and now operates as a state park.

The Douglas Mansion with the Powder Box House in front (made mostly of old TNT boxes)

Although the majority of the museum was dedicated to mining it quickly became apparent, from the placards and pictures, that when the miners got home from work they enjoyed motorcycles and cars.

I found peppered throughout the museum motorcycle and car references. One placard stated that circa 1930, thousands of automobiles were registered to the hillside city. The candid pictures of downtown in the museum centered around motorcycle clubs, and when they did not, the streets were lined with the automobiles of the time. To an auto enthusiast, these pictures are awesome.

One picture was a photo of a young man riding an Indian up the windy city road in approximately 4 inches of mud with a big grin. The first thing that struck me about the photo is the change in attitude about what constitutes a good time on a motorcycle. Could you imagine someone on a new street bike smiling as they struggled to make it through town in four inches of mud on a steep incline? On top of that, consider the ergonomics of that Indian in the mud. The throttle was on a lever, as was the gearshift, so he couldn't fully grasp the handlebars at all times. In addition the handlebars were bent back in a u shape that he held much like you would hold a suitcase you pick up at your side. The tires were narrow and not much better than bicycle tires. Yet, his smile was ear to ear. You can almost imagine the novelty and excitement of a bike with a motor when you see his smile. That's it, a bike with a motor made him happy.

I feel the majority of riders today, would be horrified to ride such a contraption, let alone in mud on a steep incline. Why? My guess is that comfort, safety and convenience have replaced, excitement, novelty, achievement and adventure.

The young men of the early 1900s, especially in mining towns & logging towns, celebrated machine conquering environment. Consider some of the races and novels of the time (all celebrated by movies now coincidently): The Great Race of cars around the world, the airplane races from England to France (as seen in Those Magnificent Men and Their Flying Machines), and Around the World in 80 Days. To see Europe at that time meant a month in a ship at the least, on top of the time it took for your sightseeing. The world was an adventure around 1900.

In comparison, our society now celebrates how easy, fast and luxurious your trip to Europe can be. Machines conquering environment are soundly looked down upon for environmental impact reasons. Even in motorcycles, comfort is celebrated; consider Harley's with their wide leather seats and back rests, reclined seating positions and windscreens.

It isn't a hard leap to assume that the miners working with mechanical tools all day (jacks, pumps, generators, elevators, rail track, engines, etc.) would be proficient with mechanical objects and might incorporate those skills into their hobbies. It's probably similar to our modern computer engineers who go home and play online (1st person shooter games, trying to take down corporate websites, or attempting to steal your bank passwords).

Outside, in the garage of the Douglas mansion, both the old man Douglas chariot (as in horses; used prominently in the film Oklahoma) and the son's pieced together pickup truck (made from an old car) still reside in the garage.

The Douglas state park also shows a video history of Jerome and a significant amount of screen time is dedicated to the hillclimb races held in the late 50's and early 60's. After a number of years, the state of Arizona rescinded their decision to allow the races due to safety concerns.

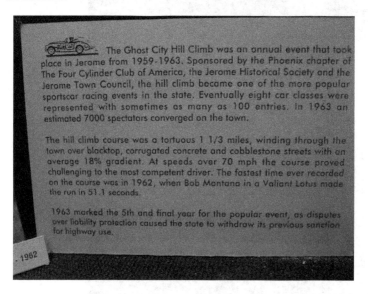

The Ghost City Hill Climb was an annual event that took place in Jerome from 1959-1963. Sponsored by the Phoenix chapter of The Four Cylinder Club of America, the Jerome Historical Society and the Jerome Town Council, the hill climb became one of the more popular sportscar racing events in the state. Eventually eight car classes were represented with sometimes as many as 100 entries. In 1963 an estimated 7000 spectators converged on the town.

The hill climb course was a tortuous 1 1/3 miles, winding through the town over blacktop, corrugated concrete and cobblestone streets with an average 18% gradient. At speeds over 70 mph the course proved challenging to the most competent driver. The fastest time ever recorded on the course was in 1962, when Bob Montana in a Valiant Lotus made the run in 51.1 seconds.

1963 marked the 5th and final year for the popular event, as disputes over liability protection caused the state to withdraw its previous sanction for highway use.

1962

Rather than attempt to describe the exciting event, I'll leave it to the internet and our instant access to information to fill that role. I found this excellent blog on the hill-climbs:

http://johnstraub.blogspot.com/2012/08/ghost-city-hill-climb-jerome-arizona.html

If you're reading this without internet access imagine pictures of 1950s sports cars flying up the side of a desert mountain road leading precariously to an old-west town hanging off a hill. Sometimes the flying was literal.

My consideration of the Ghost City races as quid essential racing cool grew exponentially as I looked at the pictures in the referenced blog. Just check out the pictures; how could you not want to be there?!

Did society gain from growing safer with actions such as ending the Ghost City races? On one hand, people that aren't racing can't get hurt racing. But on the other hand, people that crave adventure and excitement will either find it, or long for it. If a vast majority of those activities that can be used to fill that need are considered illegal, adrenalin junkies are either going to do illegal things (underground late night racing, driving recklessly on public roads, etc.) or long tensely for that excitement and adventure as they recline in their clean, comfortable, safety (perhaps causing a generation of fashion loving moody hipsters?).

But not all is lost. I'm happy to report that hillclimbs are alive and well in the Northwest where I live.

The Maryhill museum of Art allows groups to rent their hillclimb track (http://www.maryhillmuseum.org/Visit/Do/loops.html).

Also, the Northwest Hillclimb Association organizes hillclimb events around the state (http://www.nhahillclimb.org).

Both are great opportunities to enjoy an exciting event. As soon as I have a car capable of participating, I'm going to give it a shot.

Other gearhead highlights of Jerome included:

The old auto dealership has an old Plymouth jammed into it amongst the shops. As my wife purchased artisan necklaces I read through the signs on the wall chronicling the old dealership (and how they placed cars in the shop via lifts and ramps because the shop overhangs a cliff).

The mid-town museum also had more detail about the Ghost City races as well as a really cool old bicycle.

I will note, that it was interesting to me that, although the gearhead culture was one of the predominant historical references to the town of Jerome in picture, both the Douglas and mid-city museum chose to focus on the prostitution that existed in the town, although there seemed to be far fewer pictures and details available for those exhibits. It's interesting what we celebrate as a society. Also in Jerome, it seemed that in every bookstore we walked in there were novels written about, or from the point of view of, a Jerome prostitute. Yet I didn't see as much as a poem about any of the gentlemen smiling with their motorcycles, pulling their new car out of the dealership, or screaming up the hill in their Austin Healey.

I think the celebration of Jerome's prostitution, rather than the families that lived there, the churches, the car races, etc. is similar to the revisionist history we are experiencing throughout the nation. Although we all know that celebrated men who believed in God helped guide this country, now the belief in God is generally derided in film, and characters such as Billy the Kid, Bonnie and Clyde, the Texas Chainsaw Massacre, and etc. are celebrated.

I can't help that wonder if we are seeing the effects of the seeds we've sown as mass shootings rock the nation. It's foolish to be surprised when evil expands its presence when it's been celebrated. How my soul longs for men and women to know the joy, goodness, love, justice and righteousness of Christ. He stands against all that breaks your heart, and He can change those hearts that anti-depressants and counseling can't.

My apologies for the side comment, it's been tough lately to watch the news.

Back to Jerome.

At the top of the hill, the old asylum now houses both a Packard limo (with an interesting wheel chair access setup) and a Rolls Royce Phantom. Little detail is given as to why the vehicles are there, or where they came from and internet searches have provided little information. If your taste in gears expands beyond transportation, there are some neat antique clocks in the hallways of the hotel.

Packard Photos

Rolls Royce Phantom Through the Garage Doors

A local antique shop has an early 20th century gas pump decorating it's sidewalk in a patina only the Arizona desert could produce.

Also, the vehicles that are used in the city reflect the history. A local mine museum advertises with a vintage water truck. I noted a local deliveryman using a very odd, interesting flatbed Jeep I'd never seen before doing. A little internet research told me it's a FC (forward control).

If your tastes run more modern, Jerome is still the hill of choice for rich men and their exotica. I've seen more than one supercar parked along the streets of Jerome, no doubt driven up from snooty southward Scottsdale.

The city of Jerome is a fascinating place for people that enjoy machines. I'd highly recommend a visit. But the contrasts of an early 1900s mining town compared to modern America are great, and it elicits some thought.

Budget 1957 MGA Progress

Well, I finally got my head back from Portland Engine Rebuilders! Not the one on my neck but the one that sits on top of my engine block. I can't complain about the time it took though; they managed to stay within their original quote ($400) and add quite a bit of scope.

The head was tuned per the factory-tuning manual. As recommended, they cut the heart shaped metal out of the area above the piston to make it shaped like the cylinder below it; apparently this helps the fuel air mixture light when the spark from the plug ignites it. Anything to help 65 horsepower (de-rated for age)!

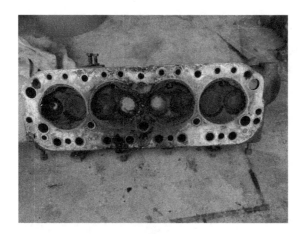

Before

After

To keep the compression the same their computer cut
the head down as the tuning manual suggested. I have

a little fear that it was cut down before and I've cut too far as I noticed one piston is different than the rest and the fan is a non-stock yellow. I think the engine might have been apart and rebuilt once before.

Portland Engine Rebuilders also did a bunch of other stuff, including replacing the springs, valve seats, etc. The full description of what they do to heads is located here:

http://www.portlandenginerebuilders.com/mshop.html

I'm trying to clean everything up as I rebuild the motor so I took the radiator out to paint, as well as try to clean up the area under it (around the steering rack). Some dry ice took the ding out of the radiator a little but not quite like it pulled the dings out of the aluminum MGB hood. Under the radiator was an inch of grease. I think the last owner/operator might have thought greasing the steering rack was done successfully by wiping a glob of grease on it, never mind the nipples for the grease gun.

I couldn't find a motor color to match the original burgundy at NAPA. I bought the darkest engine paint red and it turned out to be quite a flamboyant choice. Oh well, at least it's attractive and doesn't look like it's owner should rise to sing the Mexican national anthem during the Olympics, unlike the other paint mistake I made (more to follow on that one).

I didn't replace the rubber hoses with the factory rubber. The original hoses felt good, and as my dad pointed out, were made pre-environmentally friendly processes so they are probably massively better, but I was too concerned they'd explode at the least opportune time so I bought a long piece of hose from Napa and cut it up.

I conducted something of a science experiment. The rust on my manifold was horrific and I thought if I put it up against my new head I should be flogged (Does anyone still use this term? Maybe I should put "banned from the internet" to make it culturally relevant.) I saw online that using your battery charger and baking soda, you can remove rust from things so I decided I'd give it a try (yes, I know that there is an expensive chemical that will do the same but remember this blog is called Budget MGA).

I didn't have a good battery charger but I figured I'd need one when I was trying to get the car running so I picked up a 10 amp Die Hard charger at K-Mart for $30 bucks (on sale, go fast if you want one too). While there I saw $45 dollar type 26 batteries so I grabbed one of those too; of course I was on the motorcycle so yet again it was one heavy ride home with a battery and charger jammed in my backpack.

The science experiment worked great. I used some old sheet metal I had and a piece of fence cable to connect them to make the (anodes?). Then, I connected the negative clip straight to the manifold to make the (diode?). I placed them in a large bucket with the solution. Three hours later the rust had converted into some black hard crud. A little time in the sink with a scrub pad and it cleaned up well!

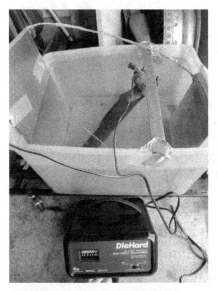

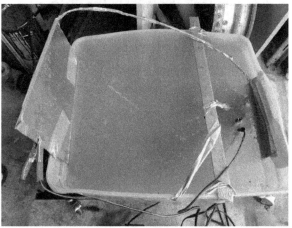

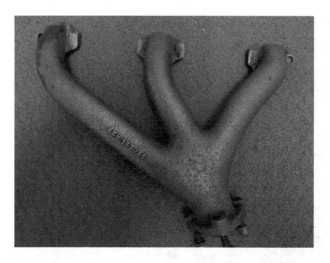

My only issue was the nice grey color I picked for manifold paint turned out to be a gaudy chrome-esque silver similar to what the Hispanics in Blythe (a very hot, very So. Cal. city I used to live in) used to paint their steel wheels to make them look chrome. In the picture below compare the cap color to the manifold color. Maybe I should paint my wheels with it! Strangely, it's the best laying high temp paint I've ever used. Some are so thin and runny but this one lays down well.

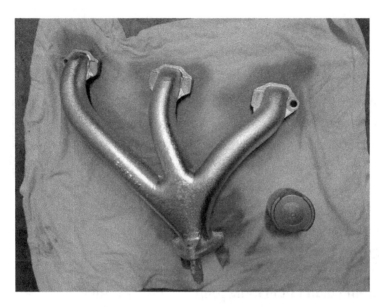

One item that is in the motor compartment that I can't seem to find a new cheap option for is the brake master cylinder. Mine is not re-buildable. I'm not sure why but it seems as though mine has been sitting on the ocean floor for 10 years. It's the only thing that was on the car that rusted up (except maybe those dang rocker panels but I'm ignoring those for now or I'd get depressed thinking about possible structural damage to the F-pillars)!

I threw an ad on Craigslist asking if anyone had one lying around they'd taken out cause it was leaking a little (hoping I could rebuild it). I received a response back from a guy saying he had one, and he'd be willing to sell it to me for $50. On top of that he had already rebuilt it but decided to go with a new one before putting it back in. Awesome. I'll pick it up tomorrow! We'll see if it works.

My wife and I went to the Moon Speed Shop open house in L.A. several weeks ago. I was stoked to see my favorite custom car shared parts with my MGA! And when I say parts, I mean the mirrors. Yes, they are the same. Outside of that nothing is the same. But I was really impressed with the car Beatnik and the builder, Gary Chopit. Gary didn't know me from Adam but was the only guy to talk to me at the show. Not only did he talk to me but also he gave me his card although it was very apparent I didn't fit in (only couple not dressed like the 50's) and probably didn't have money (I was wearing my favorite Wal-Mart car t-shirt).

Here's the site for the car:

http://www.chopitkustom.com/Beatnik/Beatnik.html

My second favorite car at the show was on the opposite end of the spectrum. Witness… well, there is no website dedicated to this one so I don't know its name. But I title it Suicide Machine because one of my friends, when he saw its pictures, called it that. I think he meant it negatively, but… what can I say. I like things most people don't.

 Next up for the MGA? Well, I'm going to sit down and
try and tune the carbs and then put them on the car.
After that I'll try and reverse the polarity (change it to

ground negative like every other vehicle on earth (right now, black is positive for you friends that don't speak car geek). Then, I'll try and start it!!!!

It probably won't start. I didn't replace the points, the starter probably needs new brushes and the alternator might be shot (I wonder if the old MGB one'll work?) but I'm going to try anyways! If it doesn't work, then I'll replace all that other stuff. I don't think I'm going to make the British show the 1st weekend in September but you never know. Anyone got a coupe windshield they want to get rid of cheap? Then, if everything else works, I might make it... maybe.

Portland Historic Races

I made it out to the Portland Historic Races on Sunday and found some fun people, great races, and hot cars. The races were held June 28th to the 30th and the featured theme was the 60th anniversary of the Corvette.

I scored a paddock (the middle of the track) pass from a buddy and was in early to get across the track before warm-ups started. The BMW CCA club was running, for charity, $5 a lap autocross. At 9 AM it was me and about two other cars running around the track with barely a break between laps. It got more popular and more people came as the day wore on and I'm willing to bet they raised a tidy sum for Take Action Inc., which provides food for at-need children on the weekend (when they can't get it at school). I was impressed; what a fun method to raise money for a charity!

The paddock area is broke down by car clubs, but because I don't belong to any of them I parked next to the autocross track by the volunteers. Wes, the friendly volunteer/car guider filled me in on the paddock drama. Apparently two clubs, which were at one point one club, are warring for members and trying schemes like parking an attractive female at the gate to direct cars to a certain paddock area. Funny stuff.

It made me wonder what happened to cause the club to split. I'm starting to realize people are people, and whether you're in a car club or church, there's likely going to be someone you don't get along with. I think you should look at the founding values to select the group you're going to hang out with, not so much the people in it. An extreme example is comparing Christians to… let's just say Hells Angels. They both likely have some morons in their group, and also some camaraderie, but one was founded by a man who loved and did the miraculous to help people (Jesus) and the other was founded by a guy who likely killed people. Why would you possibly join a group founded by a murdering desert warrior; would you be willing to support that mind set? But it's not perfectly rosy on the other side, if you're a Christian, you're still likely to find some goofs in the church. Get over it, they're everywhere, pursue the original intentions of Jesus, which are awesome, and try not to be a goof too!

I digress, but I hear too many people say they walked away from church cause of the people. That's stupid, church is God's hospital and that's like saying you can't go to the hospital cause there are sick people. But back to the race day, paddock drama aside.

It was about 10 AM but the day was already baking for Portland. With highs for the day forecasted well over 90 I think a lot of people bailed on coming out to the races. The crowds were relatively sparse. Which was great because when I headed over to the pit area I got to spend some time alone with a multi-million dollar machine (why does that sound creepy?).

I came across an Alfa Romeo 8C-35. This was one of the cars campaigned by the Alfa team when old man Ferrari wasn't old, and he managed Alfa's racing cars (before he built his own).

 The car was a piece of art and it was fascinating to walk around it and check out the brake cables, early suspension, Italian gauges, etc. I spent 10 minutes drooling on the car and the owner probably got suspicious. It was nice not to have museum barricades blocking me from looking at it. Also it seems museums always leave the hood closed too.

I later found out this car was once driven by Nuvolari, who many claim was the best driver of all time. It's now owned by Peter Giddings, who purchased the Alfa for several million. You can read more about this car at - http://petergiddings.com/Cars/TipoC50013.html

I then came across a car I'd never seen or heard of before, which is always a nice surprise. The car was a Deutsche Bonnet HBR5 – a two-cylinder car campaigned by Aurthur Cook. Later I had a chance to watch Mr. Cook race and he was subject to being lapped, repeatedly, but I give him a lot of admiration for racing something so odd and underpowered.

I also came across a Bugatti Type 35. A real one, not one of the VW motored ones! Robert Ames, just out of his race car, came over and humored our stupid questions about the hand pulleys, fuel pump, and chain adjustors for the brakes even though he was still pouring sweat!

I appreciated the time Mr. Ames took. Last year I'd approached a Mustang owner about a car whose motor had sounded especially awesome. He'd ignored me and his mechanic told me the motor was a secret (bear in mind this is historic racing, not F1). I noticed that same mustang owner had barricaded his car area with trailers this year so that even though it's an open pit, no spectators could bother him. Kinda funny, kinda sad.

Also in the pit was a dream barn find 1st generation corvette. I think I've dreamed of finding that very car in that very state. Unfortunately I couldn't find out the story because the owner was busy replacing his spindles on the XK Jaguar he was racing.

The funny thing was, this being the celebration of the 60th anniversary of the Corvette, I didn't see many other Corvettes!

One of the more affordable cars I spotted, but still desirable, was an early MGB with the pull handle doors. Clean, straight and everything an MGB should be!

I also found some oddities in the pits, including a Renault and a Crosley Hotshot. The Crosley is sprung in the rear by some beefy quarter elliptical leaf springs!

Being in the paddock also clued me in on what sort of
classic I'm likely to campaign if finances and time ever
allow. The guys with the Bugattis, Mustangs, Corvettes
and such all came in fancy trailer trucks with living areas

and pull out awnings, designed for racers. These were parked on the asphalt close to the tower. The other guys were out in the grass, off the asphalt, with old trucks and little tiny tow behind trailers with MG midgets and triumphs and other low buck racers. I have a feeling I'm destined for the grassy area.

The races were in the afternoon and a blast to watch for as long as your body could handle the sun. Many of the attendees brought large umbrellas to tie to the grandstand which I'd highly recommend.

After one race we walked back to the pits and talked to a Mr. Volstead about his ex-Jim Clark race car. One of his comments about racing the car struck me, "It's been 20 minutes and I'm still smiling"!

Being historic races there's not a ton of dicing since many of these cars are rare and/or valuable. Some of the more memorable action is when someone over-commits to a corner and ends up in the grass such as an Austin Healey did when it was chasing a Corvette with a large lead.

One of the best races was between two cars that probably don't have as much of the rare/valuable issue. The Volvo 142E of Robert Gordon and the BMW 2002 of Jeff Gerken battled it out for 2nd behind a Peter Brock replica 240Z. Gordon and Gerken were dicing hard and at points the cars appeared to be inches from each other, pushed into the grass, and stymied in the corners so hard tire haze came up from the one that had to brake. That was great to watch!

You can read more about the Peter Brock replica 240z here (I'm guessing this is the same car that won) - http://www.roadandtrack.com/special-reports/bre-nissan-370z-datsun-240z

The vendors were also out, but the consensus was there were fewer than in previous years. There were still plenty of opportunities to pick up shirts, model cars, junk food and your other typical fare. I found some great vintage racing books, which I picked up for $5.

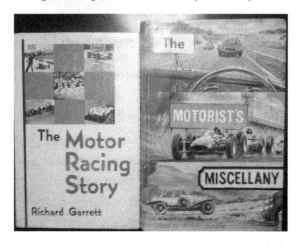

Around four the races wrapped up and people trickled out. Not all that many had made it to 4 with the heat and it being Sunday. I think everyone was happy though; the racing was good, some of the cars in attendance were exceptional, and there were other fun diversions like autocross and club gatherings.

History Repeats Itself, Broke With a 1950s Car

As my wife and I pushed my 1957 MGA back to the garage last weekend, after the fuel pump went out driving around the parking lot, I realized little has changed in terms of my cars. For the last 15 years I've been (or friends) pushing cars and I can't say that the cars have really gotten any better. I basically have the same vehicle I had at 15.

My first car was a 1951 Ford F-1 my father gave me for my 15th birthday. We drove out and bought if from a guy that my father worked with. It was beside a barn under a tree and the cab was literally filled with pack rat nest. A tree had fallen across the tailgate and the bed had rotted out but I was stoked to have a truck to restore.

We filled the tires and they held air (although rock hard). Then, in one of my proudest days, I got to steer it the 15 miles of dirt roads (the back way) home as my dad towed it.

The first job was to take the rotten bed off and my father asked me to grind the frame down to metal. I think he thought I was slacking because weeks later I still hadn't wore it down to metal although I'd been using a 6" grinder with a steel wire wheel (and of course this also started the tradition of not using a face mask;

and I wonder why I have allergy/breathing problems now). Years later I found out that they baked the paint onto these frames similar to the cast iron kitchen ovens used in the same period. That paint was probably one of the harder paint materials known to man. They should consider using it on the shuttle.

When I turned 16 I was given The Beast by my parents. This truck was an ex-electric utility pickup with a U-Haul overdriven transmission mounted to a ford straight six stacked with Carter 6-into-8 performance parts and Dana axles. And that was about it. There was a body, but not much of one, with body panels from 3 or four different trucks after the utility box was taken off. There was a hole in the door and dent in the roof from where my dad and I rolled it coming back from motorcycle riding. Yet, despite its lack of amenities, still probably my favorite vehicle I've owned and the most capable.

The day I turned 16 my buddy and I took it out to Coors canyon and grenaded the locker in the rear axle. That was a nice $800 dollar bill on day one of being legal to drive. The tone was set.

That truck also broke my hand when we came over a lip airborne out in the desert, and the wheels took a sharp turn to the right because of the force of the truck landing while they were slightly turned. My hand was in the vicinity of the steering wheel and its 100 mph spin broke one of my finger bones. The doctor put a cast on it. I took it off outside the doctor's office so I could shift to get home.

My dad still uses that truck as a wood truck. You can't kill it.

In high school I was on the lookout for a car. I saw a funny looking convertible car next to a trailer in a desert field. We saw the owner in the yard and he said we could have it for what he got it for, $30.

As we towed the car home I saw my buddy getting smaller in my rear view mirror. I pulled the truck over to watch him fly by in the melon field desperately pumping the brakes. Yeah, there were no brakes. The melons eventually stopped the car. We were a little more careful about how we connected the chains to the truck after that.

About a mile from home one of the tires disintegrated. We decided we were too close to quit. We dragged the car home on a steel wheel shooting sparks. Later I realized there were groove marks in the asphalt leading straight to the car.

It turned out it was a Kaiser Henry J someone had chopped the top off. An early monocoque (body/frame combined) with a jeep motor made in a venture by the Kaisers of ship fame after WWII.

About the same time a buddy bought a 1976 Camaro and had the prisoners paint it and put an interior in it (his dad was a warden and this was a program to teach them skills). They painted it a ghastly yellow and blue with matching interior. He got a ticket for near 100 mph with no seatbelt and needed close to a grand to pay the ticket. He was trying to sell the car and couldn't get anyone to buy it. I told him I had $1200 in my bank account and would pay him that for the car. At first he blew me off but several weeks later he told me that he'd take the $1200.

The car needed a new carb and the interior clipped in (the inmates weren't allowed to have clips so all the interior was just draped in). The Mexicans in the desert would always comment how cool the car's paint job was. Funny thing was, I never heard that from anyone not from Mexico.

That car cost me my license for a couple days. My father was at my little brothers school and heard some idiot go around the corner in front of the school with the tires broke loose and the car sliding sideways. When he looked up he saw my unmistakable blue and yellow car. In my defense, it had just rained and that was the only time I could break the tires loose in that car. I had to do it. It doesn't rain that often in the desert.

I was also told to sell the Kaiser because it wasn't good for a 16 year old to have 3 crappy cars. My mom was starting to complain that our house looked like an Indian reservation.

When I regained my license, my parents bought a Honda and decided that the old family Blazer might be a good vehicle for me. It had a new computer chip and blue-printed motor so I was game to give it a try.

I about rolled it our first night out when we came over a sand dune too fast and the backside had a cliff. We hung a wheel off but managed to get it stopped. That was an adrenaline rush!

I wanted to put a lift kit on it. Prom was coming up and it was my goal to have it lifted to do some four-wheeling in Coor's Canyon during the after party. Several days before the prom my lift kit came in.

When I was trying to get the rear spring off I was laying under the truck with my feet planted on the frame pulling on a 3 foot wrench. The wrench slipped and broke my face open. I couldn't quit because Prom was around the corner so I went in to the freezer to find something to put on it so I could continue working. I found only a biscuit. My buddy came over and was quite surprised to see a bloody raw biscuit stuck to my face. I still have the scar.

My date hated the blazer. Said it was too tall and hard to get into. Last I saw, she was in Hollywood pursuing an acting career. I like to think that I helped her realize she hated redneck and pushed her towards her city living and her chosen career.

I was 18 and whining a lot that the blazer was a family vehicle and I really wanted something more truck. My parents had always said that if I kept my grades up through high school they'd provide a vehicle and they made good on that promise. They gave me a $5k budget and we found a nice clean lifted 80's Chevy 1500 4x4 in L.A. with every extra you could think of (axle guards, tow kit, camper, camper bed kit, headers, valve covers, grille, etc.).

That truck survived my first couple years of college. There was a lot of off-roading as I went to college in Flagstaff. I even lived in it for the summer camping in the woods after my freshman year to save money for the next year. I eventually snapped the frame where the steering box bolted on and it experienced some down time.

My grandparents had an old Chevy C-10 and they were selling everything and moving to the desert in a RV. They gave me the C-10 to drive while my truck was down. It was a decently clean truck, but it did have a dent in the rear fender I put in it driving it when I was 14. It was my chore to take the lawn clippings out in the woods and dump them; coming around a corner I almost ran into another 14 year old buddy who had his own truck and I went bouncing out into a recently burned forest where I dented the fender and lived in fear of anyone discovering the dent for months.

So there I was in college with the black Chevy 4x4 and old C-10. At that time I piled a motorcycle into a tree DUI and about killed myself. I lost my full ride ROTC scholarship for "Conduct Unbecoming an Officer" but God really used that wreck to get a hold of my life which was quickly going the wrong direction.

I had to sell the C-10 to pay for the DUI lawyer. I attempted to pop the dent out of the rear fender pulling the truck over a wall mart traffic control pole (you know – the metal poles filled with concrete) and applying power. I pulled the stupid pole out of the ground and it thrashed the fender. A lot of time with a hammer after that incident.

I'd see that truck running around Flagstaff until the day I moved and each time it would make me sigh as I remembered all my stupidity.

I eventually bought the Blazer back and finished out college in the blazer. I sold the 4x4 pickup to a lesbian who loved it because it was a "man truck".

After college I decided to head for Hawaii. God really opened the door. I googled "Construction in Hawaii" and called the first job I could find a phone number for. It turned out they had won a court case that day to continue and needed a project engineer. I struck out for Hawaii without a car and my parents bought the Blazer back.

My first truck in Hawaii was a total disaster. I found another Ford straight six but a 1980's two wheel drive this time. I bought the truck in Hilo at about 8 PM (after work I rode over from Kona), on the rainy side of Hawaii. I hit a puddle on the way home and lost the rotten exhaust. I spent 20 minutes kicking it out from under the truck because it'd jammed under the axle.

About halfway home the headlights started dimming, coming back, dimming, etc. Then the truck died. Of course by this time it was one in the morning and I was on the military reservation with signs everywhere "Absolutely No Stopping" and it was freezing cold on the mountain. Around 2 A.M. a MP pulled up and called a tow truck.

I found out the next day that the alternator was loose. On top of that, the brake lines had rusted through under the bed and I had been driving with only front brakes (that little pressure check valve works!)

I painted that truck flat black with white inserts. My buddies called it the penguin truck.

I sold that truck to some local landscapers and bought a lifted F-150 with the 5.0 motor. The bed bolts had rusted out around 3 of the four bolts and every time I hit a bump the bed would bounce up and down. This was particularly noticeable because in Hawaii I often had people riding in the back on the way to surf spots. I'd yell back, "keep your legs away from the bolts, it'll pinch like hell!"

The radiator on that truck was terrible and I'd often arrive at my destination in a cloud of steam.

My father took pity on me and sold me his truck for $2500. A straight 71 Ford Highboy with a 390. It cost me 1500 to get it to Hawaii but I had a big block classic 4x4!

The Ford served well for about a year and then developed a deathly knock that continues to this day despite thousands I've dropped on the top end (turns out it's a bottom end problem). Between buying it shipping it to Hawaii and the top end work I've spent over $6000. Sad considering you can buy them here in Oregon for $1500.

The construction boom fell away and I ended up back in the states.

I eventually got a job in downtown Portland and the people flipping me off or asking me if I needed a fire extinguisher in the smoking, knocking truck eventually got old. A friend was selling a Taurus for a grand and I bought it. I told myself it didn't matter. A car is a car if all you are using it for is transportation.

... But eventually I wanted to date again and decided that a car was not always just a car. For the price of a Taurus about the only thing interesting I could buy (that ran) was an MGB. So I sold the Taurus and bought a barely running MGB. The first night my roommate had to push it several times as we tried to figure out why it would die when we turned the headlights on (alternator again).

I loved my MGB. I eventually converted it from a rubber bumper with steel wheels to a chrome bumper with wire wheels. You can see more of that project at www.budgetmgb.blogspot.com.

I married my wife in that car, autocrossed it and thoroughly enjoyed it. But then one day I saw an MGA. And I had to have one.

After months of searching I found one for about what I could get out of the MGB.

And here I am today. 15 years later I'm back to a 1950's car that I had to drag home. It's almost depressing how little I've improved. Those that fail to learn from their mistakes are doomed to repeat them. I guess I'm not learning from my mistakes.

I'd just got the MGA running and was testing it in the apartment parking lot when the fuel pump died. I'm hoping to, by the end of the summer, autocross the car. It's my goal. Wish me luck. And pray that I can progress in my cars beyond broken 1950s rusty hulk, it's been 15 years and I'm ready to move on to a working 1950s car.

How To Not Be Bored At Car Shows

I've had the pleasure of attending two excellent car shows in the last 3 weeks and I've come to the conclusion that if you don't talk to the owners you are missing out. The stories behind some of these cars bring them to life, and without the stories I just get bored as I see another Camaro/Mustang/Chevelle/etc.

I wanted to share some of these stories with you because I think they're very engaging and they're what I am wish was in more car magazines. I get so bored reading about the tech info on the restoration. I don't care what duration cam you used, I want to know if the grinder went through your leg causing 8 stiches!

I wasn't taking notes when I talked to these guys, and a week or two have passed so forgive me if the stories are just a little off; remember the telephone game?

The owner of the below Chevelle has put 100 miles on the car since finishing his 7 year restoration. For 7 years this car was a garage ornament. I applaud his patience. Can you imagine his joy the first time he got to drive it? He hasn't even really set the rings yet. I bet he gets a big ol' smile the first time he gets to put his foot to the floor. I'm fighting to restore my MGA and I just don't have that sort of patience. And the end result will probably show that his car is much nicer than mine. Nice work!

This fastback mustang was driven to the show by the parents of the owner (since new). I've seen them several times and talked with them and they always mention that their son is "busy today". They are so proud of the car though. You can see it's a reflection of their pride in their son, and even if he's too busy to be with them today, at least they get his car which reminds them of him.

The below mustang was brought to the show by two ladies in memory of their late husbands who built this car and another. I didn't actually talk to them about it because the topic was a little... maybe sensitive... for my comfort but I thought it was touching. I also thought it was funny that they chose to place roosters in the seats; I wonder if they were, in a good natured way, representing their husbands in a humorous manner.

This MR2 is my buddy Andrew's car. Andrew's fit an aftermarket turbo with 18 lbs. of boost into this car. He let me drive it once, and when the turbo kicks in you need to make sure you have the wheels pointed the right direction. I'd never experienced turbo pull like that before and I now understand why all the hot rodders are ditching their superchargers for twin turbos. What a rocket!

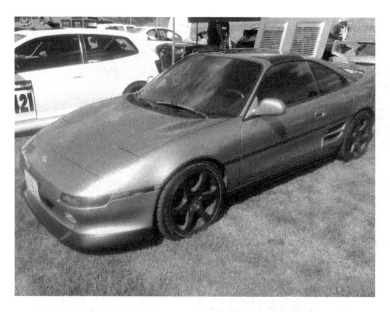

The owner of this 240z with a giant Ford motor talked cars with me for a long time. Even though I had one of the ugliest cars at the show, he came over and hung out with me talking about British cars he's owned. I think he got bored with British power. He obviously decided to go the Carol Shelby/Sydney Allard direction and jam an American motor into a foreign car that can turn corners. He says it's well sorted and sticks to the ground on the autocross track. That's gotta be fun!

This shopping cart custom is a great example of a story that needs to be told. The owner wasn't by the car so I couldn't ask... why? But I wanted to know. I'm guessing epic late night hill runs, possibly ending with road rash. Ah, youth. I sometimes miss my college late nights.

The below truck is just awesome. A couple of brothers that go to the local church built this and a bunch of other contraptions. I love it. It reminds me of the stories my dad tells about the early 80s and the ridiculous car projects they built because parts were cheap and plentiful. It's great to see young guys that are still having fun with cars, even if they're the last of a dying breed. I hope they're not. I think autos are way better than P.C.s or Xbox. If nothing else, at least to enjoy them you have to be outside in the real world. Make sure you note the vice grips and tie straps holding parts of this truck together.

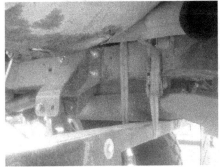

Both events were hosted by local churches and both were exceptional. I thought it was funny when a church service ended one of the shows in front of the MGA. It was the first church service the MGA has attended!

I applaud the churches for putting such effort into reaching out to the gearhead community. Free food, bands, 50's DJ's, awards, silent auctions; these churches went all out. My heart hopes that the shows brought someone closer to knowing the love of Christ; I can't imagine going through life without knowing the Savior. And funny as it sounds, when you have the knuckle bashing curse inducing hobby of car restoring, it sure is a nice change to take a shower and go be around some great people at a good church. I pity the guys that don't get to do that, they're missing out. There's only so much knuckle bashing someone can take before they get that sour puss car owner look. Car guy? Live in the Portland area? Maybe try one of these car show churches, you might enjoy it!

The below shot of me in the 'vette is cheesy, but I appreciated that the sign in the front of his car said something to the effect of, "Climb in, take pictures!" instead of "DON'T TOUCH!!". I voted best of show for this car simply because of the sign. Funny thing was, the corvette steering wheel hit my thighs and I'm not a big guy. I prefer the MGA's layout!

If you want the younger generation to be interested in these cars, let them sit in them. Let them smell the leather. Let them feel the wheel and the gear shift. Let them drive them. If you just ask them to look at them at car shows, of course they'll be bored. They don't know that the car can give them adrenaline and a sense of freedom when they step on the gas. You do, that's why you paid so much money to have it. Your frame of reference is different and you need to share your positive experiences with the younger generation or they're going to think old cars simply means sitting around fields trying to win trophies (BORING!).

Here's another one where I wanted a story. I've never seen a truck Corvair, but alas, the owner was not camped out with the truck. How cool is this pickup though?!

When I engaged the owner of the below Chevy station wagon, he hold me that this car won custom car of the year in the late 90's. I would have never known if he hadn't told me. We also started talking about the price of chroming. It's disgusting! The front bumper, to get it perfect, cost him $3k back then. He said now, probably $6k. Someone needs to invent a cheaper chroming process! And I mean chrome, not the plastic paint the Malaysians put on so many of my MGA parts.

This Chevelle was interesting because the story was posted right at the front of the car. Because hot rods were (mostly) a young man's thing in the 60's, and there was a war going on, it's not a story I haven't heard before but it is well worth the read and reminder. Take a minute and read the plaque.

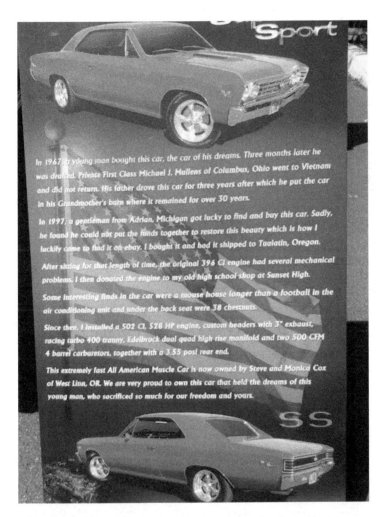

In 1967 a young man bought this car, the car of his dreams. Three months later he was drafted. Private First Class Michael J. Mallens of Columbus, Ohio went to Vietnam and did not return. His father drove this car for three years after which he put the car in his Grandmother's barn where it remained for over 30 years.

In 1997, a gentleman from Adrian, Michigan got lucky to find and buy this car. Sadly, he found he could not put the funds together to restore this beauty which is how I luckily came to find it on ebay. I bought it and had it shipped to Tualatin, Oregon.

After sitting for that length of time, the original 396 CI engine had several mechanical problems. I then donated the engine to my old high school shop at Sunset High.

Some interesting finds in the car were a mouse house longer than a football in the air conditioning unit and under the back seat were 38 chestnuts.

Since then, I installed a 502 CI, 528 HP engine, custom headers with 3" exhaust, racing turbo 400 tranny, Edelbrock dual quad high rise manifold and two 500 CFM 4 barrel carburetors, together with a 3.55 posi rear end.

This extremely fast All American Muscle Car is now owned by Steve and Monica Cox of West Linn, OR. We are very proud to own this car that held the dreams of this young man, who sacrificed so much for our freedom and yours.

The below Porsche sure was pretty and I thought it was excellent that it still had its tool kit. When I was talking to the owner about it, he told me it was his father's car. That's got to be pretty fun, having your dad's old car. My dad had a Corvette red 1966 Chevelle. If I was driving it now, I'd have a car that looked an awful lot like the Chevelle above. I wouldn't complain!

One of my favorite guys there was the below old guy, who brought an ancient truck and tractor combo. It wasn't because he brought them, but because he fired the John Deere up for everyone that I really appreciated his setup. Well, that and the fact that he's at an age where many people have retired to the home and he's still building projects. I hope I can be more like this if I make it to that age.

The below Porsche was another one owner car. On the
rear view mirror he had his name printed onto a piece

of label maker tape. When I asked him why he stared at me for a couple seconds and then said, "Well,... I can't remember". That's a long relationship with a car!

Well, those are just some of the stories that I can remember and have pictures for. There were others I heard and can't remember now, or ones that I wish I knew but couldn't find an owner. But the moral of this story is, when you're at the car show, talk to the owners. Find out why they built the car. Ask what they love about it. You may find that the car show becomes much more interesting than when you were only concerned about how nice the paint looks and how big the motor is.

The MGA is Legal and Racing Season is Starting!

Short update tonight as I'm tired; it's been a great racing filled weekend but I don't want to stay up until one in the morning writing tonight. The main point of this update is the above picture which makes me a very happy camper indeed. I've got plates for the MGA and I didn't have to get any funky door tags or lien titles!

About 3 weeks after submitting my registration to DMV I get a call from Bob who tells me that he's "the one that decides whether you get your title". I was a little taken aback that Oregon's bureaucratic process comes down to some guy named Bob calling me on the phone to grill me but I went with it.

After a full court press where Bob repeatedly asked me if I was "sure" there was no license plate or registration in the car, I finally communicated that it was a project car without much of anything when I got it. Bob started asking questions and once he figured out that I knew this MG inside and out he revealed to me that he used to have an MGB.

Bob then proceeded to tell me tales of his MGB including how he used to blast between L.A. and San Diego at 130 MPH. Thinking an MGB doing 130 MPH was pure b.s., I made a small comment that he "must have had overdrive" but quickly let it go remembering that Bob was "the one that decides whether you get your title".

Bob eventually said that he thought he would recommend me for my title.

This is yet another example of why having an MG rocks. People have a strange liking for them that transcends reason. I hear about people with Porsches who often return to their car to find spit on their seats. I wonder if I was restoring a 911 if Bob would have still recommended me.

The metal work is ongoing. I cut out all the soft spots or holes that the grinder with the wire wheel found. Then I've started welding everything back together. Inside the boxes I'm using rustoleum BBQ paint because it's only $5 a can but doesn't light on fire when welded on.

My metal bandsaw blade broke after a year of use. I went down to Lowe's and bought the $10 Bosch metal band saw blade. It worked great for about two cuts. Then it strangely would cut nothing but an arch no matter how I moved the metal. After cutting out several dangerous curved daggers I googled it and it turns out that if the teeth are eaten off of one side of the blade it will cut nothing but curves. Sure enough, upon close inspection, a fair chunk of teeth were missing.

I ordered a new blade and I've been waiting (im)patiently for it to arrive. It finally came on Friday but the Oregon Trail Rally was at the Portland International Raceway Friday night, and an autocross outing for the car group I'm involved with (Gearheadz Portland) Saturday at the awe inspiring parking lot of the old lumber yard in Packwood Oregon, ate up the last day and a half and I haven't had time to dig back in on the MGA.

The rally Friday night was fun and as always I was inexplicably drawn to the older cars. I stopped by the gentleman driving the Saab Sonnet and asked him how he liked the car. He replied "it's a pain to get in and out of".

I laughed, thinking he was joking but then he said, "I've even tried to lose a couple pounds but it hasn't helped." I think he was serious.

The Saab did well and I saw it run late into the evening. The same can't be said for the other piece of classic exotica I saw. I think this was the first Lancia Fulva I've ever seen in person. It looked impressive but again the owner didn't seem too enthused. I asked him about the motor and he said, "It's basically a Fiat". Replying that I heard they weren't super reliable he responded, "Yeah, it's basically not as reliable as the rest of them."

Poor guy, I didn't mean to hurt his feelings. I felt even worse when I saw it only in the first stage. Hopefully I didn't jinx him and I simply missed him on the other stages.

The next day, the Pacwood Washington autocross was amazing. Tucked into an epic valley surrounded by beautiful mountains lies the largest parking lot I've ever seen without light poles or planters. It's a little poignant that the saw mill is gone, but what an autocross track. I was helping others and only hitched a ride along for a single run, but I'm really looking forward to the day I get to drive up there. It was awesome.

Our car group had a great time and as pit crew I gained some experience. After one lap my buddy discovered his fenders were digging into the tire so we quickly jacked the car up and pulled out the hub spacers. The next lap we figured out his turbo intercooler fan wasn't spinning so we quickly hard wired the fan to the power. It was kind of fun. I might enjoy pit crewing (as long as I still got to do some driving sometimes).

Another highlight of Pacwood was standing on the track (cone duty) while the Nissan GT-R ran around. We nicknamed it Godzilla because it was monstrous; so loud, so fast, somewhat large (compared to a Miata) and mean. A very cool car.

I was impressed with the new little Subaru BRZ although I didn't get a pic. I also stopped by the Scion booth at the rally and picked up the low down on this little car. What a fun little purpose built average man track access car. I hope it's wildly successful.

As for the MGA, I'm hoping tomorrow I can start closing those boxes up, finish up welding on the main body, and start getting some Rustoleum paint on the main body and the backside of the fenders. Next weekend I'll have most of Saturday and Sunday to get the body panels back on.

First Rally for the MGA!

In my industry we're not allowed to recover costs on a new project until it is "used and useful"; this week the MGA became used and useful and I started recovering some of my effort with good times. Myself, a buddy, and the MGA participated in our first time, speed, distance (TSD) rally.

The story doesn't start there though. First I had to prepare for the event.

The MGA, recently registered, still wasn't quite ready for a rally. What was lacking most was a speedometer/odometer. Realizing it would take an act of God as a tailwind to make the MGA speed, I wasn't overly concerned with this before the concept of being evaluated on time and distance came up. Also, the pending purchase of a home, with its associated down payment, had pretty much killed all non-essential spending like speedometer cables.

I ordered a speedometer cable as soon as the budget allowed (June 1st). It of course arrived the day before the rally (or night as I had to work all day and can't collect the mail until 6 PM).

Taking the old speedometer cable out I realized that it was only broken at the very end and the housing was in great shape. I thought maybe I could just slide the new cable in to the old housing and call it good. Of course the new cable is a good 4 inches longer than the old one so that failed.

When trying to put the new cable and housing in, it was way too long so now it's routed in S shapes all around my engine bay, under dash and below the car. Then the best part: the part that screws into the speedometer was too large and wouldn't fit through the firewall hole. The old one disconnected to allow the cable to slide through the firewall. The new unit was crimped on. Rather than drilling a new hole (because there were also wires going through it that I didn't feel like disconnecting and re-routing while I drilled), I un-crimped the end of the cable and slid it through.

Re-crimping was moderately successful. It was very apparent I didn't have the right tool. I couldn't squeeze too hard or the cable couldn't spin in the housing.

Old Cable End

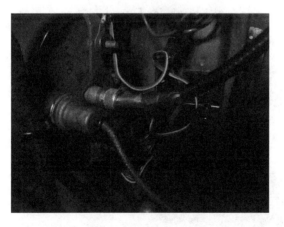

New Cable End (Yes that's Duck Tape)

By this time it's 8:30 to 9 PM. I take the car out for its first drive and the odometer still doesn't work. After jacking the car up and rechecking the transmission attachment, I realize that yes, the cable is appropriately attached and it's the speedometer that's not working.

A quick google search leads me to believe the gauge itself is sticking. Big surprise, the gauge read 10,450 miles and there's every chance that it's been broke since circa 1958.

I tried to take the speedometer apart but that's impossible without taking the needle off, which effectively kills your calibration unless you're really lucky putting it back together. I did my best by spraying Brakeklean and then penetrating oil into the housing.

It was approaching 1030 and I finally get the odometer to slowly react to speed, although far from real time.

Picture of the Speedo after the Rally (note: it worked 90 miles!)

Bear in mind I have to go in early to work the next day to get off early for the rally. At this point I still had to put together my tool box, and rallying materials. I made it to bed well past 11 to be up at 530.

My navigator was to be a good buddy, Michael, who will be moving to the East Coast soon so I thought this'd be a fun way to hang out before they go.

We headed out to the rally somewhat concerned that if there was a tight tech inspection my car would fail. Yes, the mechanicals should be solid after all the work I've done, but there are little things that a picky person could claim as unsafe. For example: there are no door seals so the doors jiggle a little, the door handles are held on by zip ties for the time being (until I get the door panels refinished and back on), the brakes, although strong, are a ways down the pedal swing, and significant portions of the body are missing from when I tried to get rid of the significant cancer (there are no rocker panels, & holes in the bottoms of fenders). I personally don't feel that any of the above things are really a risk to safety but it never ceases to amaze me what our bubble boy culture worries over these days.

Our first breath of relief came at the start of the rally. Our race coordinator did not seem to be a prude and the inspections were self-certification. Yes, it has tires and stops; thank you for not being a jerk (I get the impression some tech inspectors own a fancy car and can't understand why I don't)!

At the Lowe's Parking Lot Start

The first task was to digest the 15 page rule book in 20 minutes. I left this to the navigator as I could then blame all delays on him. This may have factored in to the story that follows.

After an odometer check section, the race started at a fire station near Damascus Oregon. Because we'd showed up very early to get the lowdown on how to rally, we were the first out of the gate.

The first instruction, from the fire station, read "proceed the way you came out of the parking lot". We headed out left on the highway the direction we came in. There were some other words in that paragraph but we didn't want to overload ourselves right out of the gate so we barreled on.

Soon, nothing made sense in the following instructions. About 5 minutes down the road we realized we had to have went the wrong direction. We re-read the paragraph and realized that the "proceed the way you came…" referred to the driveway of the fire station, and later the paragraph told us to turn right, not left out of the driveway.

On top of that, the speedometer hung lifeless at zero.

I pulled to the side of a narrow two lane road with ditches on either side, the MGA hanging 3 feet out into the road. Soon I was buried under the dash with my feet sticking out into the road as I struggled with the speedometer cable that had, of course, un-crimped itself. I soon became aware of the feeling of wind as many cars passed my toes. Turns out this particular country road was a busy country road. Fearing for my life, or at least my bottom half, I moved the car down the road to an outlet and resumed the battle with the speedometer cable.

Seconds Before my Head Was Under the Dash

5 minutes later, with the speedometer cable (barely) back in place, we tore off down the road to resume the rally. The speedometer begrudgingly followed behind our current trajectory by several seconds and reported in vagaries; better than nothing!

Our theory was, if we were out of the station first, if we passed everyone (of course doing the speed limit; the rally instructions are always under the speed limit) we'd be back in place. I must admit, this was one of the more fun times we had during the rally.

At one point, when we realized everyone else was going the opposite direction, I spun it wide open (all 70 horsepower), sideways, through a deserted gravel parking lot. Yeehaw! I hope my passenger had fun as well; years in the desert sliding trucks taught me a lot about over-steer slides and I can come out of them about wherever I want. I haven't dealt with under-steer much though, and in another similar lot (yes, we were a total lost joke) the front end just kept pushing until finally I could get the rear end to come around; the A needs more power to the rear axle so I can swing it better!

At another point, after a particularly deep dip and then bump, my navigator remarked, "Well, that's the first time I've ever been airborne in a rally".

We eventually ended up in the boondocks going down an awesome road but we were somewhat concerned that we hadn't seen another rally car in quite a while. But what a road; sudden 10 foot drops with short radius corners in them made for a great time.

Eventually we admitted our total dumb-founded-ness and called in to the rally coordinator to beg for help.

We then learned a key lesson: at T intersections, you are supposed to turn left (unless otherwise specified). You DO NOT read on to the next instruction to see which way to turn.

Eventually, we made it to the first checkpoint when we were supposed to be crossing it the second time. Legs one and two were logged as Did Not Finish (DNF) for us.

But legs 3 and 4 we nailed. We were a couple minutes off but we didn't max out on score (in other words, we were within an acceptable range). Turns out that turning left at Ts was a major component.

And what beautiful country and great roads they picked! We were cruising some single lane back roads that twisted and turned through some breathtakingly beautiful Oregon scenery. I challenge you that there's not a more beautiful place on Earth in the summer evening. Weather was 60 degrees, the sunset was orange, the evergreens were dark, the farm fields were perfectly maintained on rolling hills bordered by imposing forests, the aging barns adorned the skyline with dignity, and life was perfect running down the road in a rally with my 1957 MGA at twilight.

And the oil pressure stayed up and the temperature stayed down; good girl MG!

Michael and I had a lot of laughs that night. Whether it was me running from my restroom break in the blackberry bushes to barely make it out of a checkpoint at the right time, or him discovering the flashlight he'd been juggling was totally pointless because there was a light for rally navigation factory mounted on the dash in front of him, we had a great time.

We ended the rally at about 930 or 10 and loved it. The end stop is a pizza joint and everyone gets to talk about where they screwed up and their little adventures. I saw a lot of smiles.

I can't wait to do it again!

I'm also hoping I can manage to pass an autocross tech inspection soon as well; more to come hopefully!

The All British Field Meet

I drove my MGA out to the Portland All British Field Meet this weekend. Because it's about a 45 minute drive from my house, I could have been high from the long exposure to burning oil smoke but I had a great time. There weren't as many eye catching oddities as I thought there'd be but there were a few I thought I'd share.

The sun coming up over the tented Range Rovers was a great sight. I would love to have one of these someday. What a fun rig!

A Bentley caught my attention for quite a while. There's just something about old Bentley cars that make them one of the quid-essential in my book. It's probably just because I read The Wind in the Willows too many times and Mr. Toad is one of my favorite literary characters. I wonder where Bentley went so wrong; they look like pimped out Chryslers now.

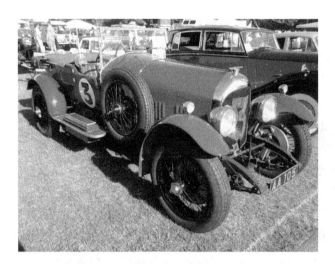

If you take a look at my picture of the "suspension" you realize there can't be much because I can't imagine that brake line running from the frame to the wheel assembly has much flex.

Is there a better looking motor than an e-type? You've gotta love the polished valve cover and fuel injection on this one.

MGs dominated the show. A really strong showing. If you have any questions about your MG restoration I'm sure you can find great advice here.

The car below was runner up for best in show. The honors couldn't have went to a nicer guy as Craig Cootsona was glad (literally) to answer questions and brought a stack of build sheets to handout if anyone wanted to copy his techniques/vendors/parts. He said he's been working on this car since 2004 and just 6 weeks ago they "finished" it. He's been building it with his father who was also in attendance.

Over at the track the Sovren vintage racers were having a blast. Well, hopefully they were. In comparison with other races, like the Oregon Trail Rally, these guys have no crowds, often get taken off the track for cars dying/running off the road, don't dice it up much, and have to race in groups with a number of other classes because there's not enough people to field many of the classes. I'd still do it, but I'm not sure it's the most fun racing. My friends that compete in the Pro3 (1990s 3 series BMW) class seem to have a lot of fun and do more actual racing.

In the area for "Other Marques" a few rarities (at least in the states) were in attendance. I can't recall ever seeing any of the 3 cars below before.

Inside a big Rolls Royce someone had taken great pains to be as historically accurate as possible, placing a bottle of Grey Poupon on the rear seat's shelf.

In the British car magazines you read often about how fun, and quick the Lotus Elan's are. You don't realize why until you're standing next to one. These cars are tiny and make the twin cam four mounted in it look big, especially with massive side-draft carbs.

Some fine Austin Healeys also helped fill the field.

A little red racer looked like a lot of fun!

Pat Moss' rally car was in attendance! Pat Moss was so
fast she would beat the men flat out and take 1st place.
I think it's funny to hear about Danica Patrick, like its
some great movement for women when she's got
nothing on Pat Moss 40 years ago. These women (Pat
and her navigators) were classy too! I've read that their
appearance was important to the factories image so
they'd quickly clean up at checkpoints to make sure
they looked good when their pictures were being taken.

Ok, after ogling this car for at least 10 minutes I got to talk to the owner. He admitted he was buffaloing me and this car was just a beat up old Healey he bought for $9500 and didn't want to spend $20k restoring. I'm impressed. He did a great job recreating a beat up rally car!

There were some fine looking big cats (Jaguars) in attendance too.

And again, I couldn't help taking a picture of an E-Type motor.

This little MGC was the only MG in attendance wearing the hard top. These hard tops are great and compliment the MGB shape well. I'd even go out on a limb and say MGBs look best with these tops on.

The cleanest MGB in attendance was a nice little blue one with a supercharger. A really clean car!

As an MGA owner, I'm naturally drawn to them and there were some great examples in attendance.

Elvas were built with MGA motors but had upgraded suspension and a fiberglass body. The body shape is unique and may not be for everyone but, unless Elva got the suspension geometry completely wrong, they must be fun to drive.

One of the most impressive cars in attendance was this all original 2nd owner (same family) car. The original owner used this car hard. The current owner (a nephew) has 10 boards full of rally pins. Great to see! The owner says he's continuing to rally it in the Klamath Falls area.

What I want to know is, where is the dealership to test drive these little Morgans?!

Hiding over with the Jaguars was an early MG. In my opinion, way cooler than even my MGA.

Sunday morning kicked off the swap meet. Kellie and I brought down some of the junk laying around my garage and made our gas money back for the two days!

The cars for sale seemed to be going fast and there were some neat ones to buy. The British pickup below was my favorite being offered. I've never seen anything quite like it.

This MGA parts car was going for a grand!

This sprite had been there minutes when a sold sign was put on its windshield.

I came out pretty well, found some stuff I needed for a total of $57. Can't get much for $57 these days!

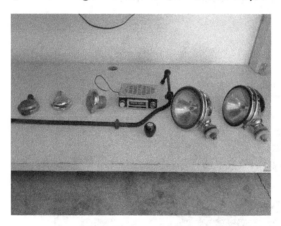

The 2013 All British Field meet was a great success with a lot of interesting and great looking cars attending. Throw in some racing action and a swap meet and you've got a great weekend. I also didn't manage to get pictures of the many events that were for charity (autocross, slalom and Range Rovers giving rides through the motocross track) but they added a touch of class to the event. In comparison to the American hot rod shows, there is an air of bravado that is missing at these British events, for better or worse. Old Nigel just doesn't have the same attitude as the American's raised in the sixties. Somehow this equates to cars that turn, instead of going fast in a straight line... and less Harley t-shirts/vesties (score a big point for the British on the last one).

1st Autocross Races!

The MGA participated in several autocross races in the last two weeks and despite its loose handling and need for a sway bar it's a complete blast to autocross. We even threw in a rally just to make things even more fun.

The first autocross was at the Portland Historic Races. The funny thing is, I know I spent time during the week leading up to it getting the car ready but for the life of me I can't remember what I did. I do remember that I found that my custom bumper setup was getting loose and I had to re-affix it. Not a big surprise considering the jerry rigging I used to get it on.

I experimented with bolting on just the over-riders in an ode to a Cobra. But, in its current condition the over-riders just make it look like a toothless hillbilly who enjoyed Copenhagen (chewing tobacco) too long.

I showed up early for the Historics Races and was lucky to share the autocross track with about 3 other guys when it opened at 9 AM. Later in the day I'd see about 20 cars lined up for it at any one time. The autocross is a $5 per lap "run it as you brung it" event, with the proceeds going to charity. I love this charity idea, and I wish more people would host charity autocrosses!

The MGA caused quite the stir. I saw people whipping out their camera phones and walking down from the club area to watch me autocross. I don't think a lot of people have seen an MGA autocross, let alone such an ugly one.

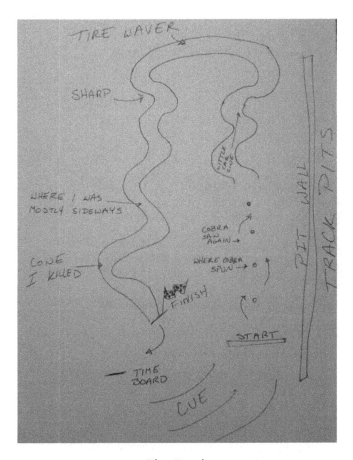

The Track

The MGA didn't disappoint as a spectacle I'm sure. As I headed out on my first lap I found out quickly that the skinny tires and lack of sway bars makes for a sliding, leaning, squealing ride. The track was a blast, well-marked and tight. I think the MGA remained sideways for a quarter of it as it slid from corner to corner with one tire in the air desperately trying to find pavement to apply power to. The good news was, the slide was surprisingly easy to control, much like a truck on a cinder road.

The oil pressure stayed up and the temperature stayed down. My old MGB would get pretty warm during autocross runs. The MGA seems to stay cooler which is surprising.

After my 3rd run the track coordinator ran over and told me that the race announcer was an MGA owner and when he heard I was running one around the autocross track like a maniac he wanted to buy me a run. My fourth run was on the announcer!

After the fourth run my right front shock was squeaking
so I headed back to the parking area.

I saw a Cobra heading toward the track with a full roll
bar and racing style seat that extends out past the
helmet which led me to believe it was quite the
autocrosser. I decided to stick around and watch it
race.

The Cobra seemed to cautiously leave the start gate.
Next out of the gate was a slalom. The Cobra must have
tapped his throttle too hard because almost instantly he
spun a 360. He started forward again but at the next
cone it happened again, spin. He then appeared to give
up and idle around the track. Apparently you can have
too much power for autocross.

I also watched a Ferrari from the 80's take on the track. I knew they were slow, but what no one mentions is how good they look going slow. I'd still trade an underpowered Ferrari for the MGA. There's just something about a prancing horse.

The world is getting small. I took a look at my phone about this time and noticed on Facebook that my buddy had tagged me in a photo of the MGA racing that one of the spectators took.

Upon inspection back home the shock didn't appear to be blown out. I topped off the oil (it was quite a bit low) and sprayed PB Blaster on all the bushings to try and reconstitute the rubber a little. It seemed to work, no more squeak.

I also wanted to address the other annoying habit of the MGA before the SCCA autocross the next weekend, fearing it would ban me from competition. Much like an embarrassing dog, the MGA likes to leak on everything. Oil is sailing past the old rings and is pushed out the tappet air vent on the side of the motor. Everywhere the MGA idles, it marks its territory with 20-50w oil. I find myself not parking near the homes of people I like for fear of embarrassment.

I designed what I call a "diaper". Really, it's just an oil catch can for the tappet vent.

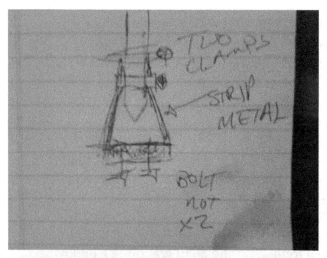

The Friday night before a Sports Car Club of America autocross there was a Cascade Car Club rally and I decided to try my luck and do both back-to-back. If you own a Miata, this probably wouldn't be a cause for any concern. A 1957 MGA is a slightly different animal.

That's an exciting 24 hours for a car just recently restored to the street.

The rally went down without incident. We were thrown for a good loop in one leg by an out of order numbering on the instructions that we missed. All other legs we posted a time for though! A marked improvement over our last rally.

One of the things I enjoy most about the rally is getting out and enjoying the gorgeous Oregon back country from winding roads as the sun sets on warm summer days. I don't think I'd be into TSD rallies at all if they were run in an urban environment.

And the oil pressure stayed up and the temperature stayed down again. One of the brakes started squeaking and the wheel/drum was a little hot. We were braking hard, a lot, as we sailed past turns we should have taken.

At the post-race dinner a controversy brewed with the participants that a route instruction based on a road sign had a possible dual meaning. When we turned in our time sheet the scrutineers asked which of the two actions we took at the sign. It was somewhat embarrassing to admit, "Neither, we were just glad to see the sign because it meant we were on the right road for once".

I got home and loosed the brake adjustment back up, checked the oil (down a quart) and replaced the diaper. It appeared to do its job well as it was filled with oil.

It was time for bed and five hours of sleep before heading to my next race.

The tech inspection at SCCA autocross events is thorough and I was somewhat concerned. Mechanically I believe the car is sound, but the body looks far from. I worried that perhaps someone would deny me access to the track based on missing body panels or door fit. It was funny, standing in line to get my tech card I heard many other people with similar concerns such as, "I wonder if tech will give me a hard time for all the stereo speaker wires laying loose in my trunk". I wonder how much anxiety has been wasted on worrying about stupid little things for autocross tech inspections.

The inspectors took a look at the mechanical portions of my car, and then complimented it. There was no mention of my body. I wasted some worry.

I had several friends racing that day, and even one that came out to ride along, which always makes car events more exciting. The older I get, the more I prefer friends to be involved in my activities and the more willing I am to try and make them a part of them.

The track was fun, but for some reason it didn't quite induce the same adrenalin as the one at the historic races. I can't help but wonder if that was my own doing because I stayed up too late.

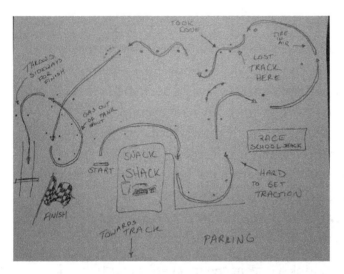

My diaper wearing car embarrassed me again with its leaky tendencies. My buddy pulled his red car behind mine and when I fired mine up, it blew a spackle of oil across his lower front end.

Other than its tendency to piddle on things, I was proud of the MGA. She ran great, and again didn't get hot, even when driven in anger for almost a minute. On this track the body roll was less pronounced than the previous week's, and I was only four seconds behind my buddies Miata with a 49 second best lap (his was 45). Another one of our friends from our church car group (GearheadzPortland@blogspot.com), who's qualified and competed at the national level, was running just over 40.

Considering I have drum brakes, lever action shocks, a live rear axle and no sway bars, I'm not disappointed with my times (except the lap where I lost the track). Compare my MGA hardware to the Miatas which have disc brakes, telescoping shocks, independent rear suspension and sway bars. I was proud of my old girl and her performance.

Over on the track we could see they were racing open wheel cars. I had to fight a nagging little voice that was saying, "if you were a real man, you'd be out there and not putzin around the parking lot in 1950's technology (well... it's British so its probably 1930's technology)."

The reality is I'd probably be out there but I still haven't invented that thing or started my business as I don't think the electric utility paycheck will ever pay for that. Non-union utility paychecks barely cover 1950s technology racing autocross. It might have 15 years ago. Thank you world leaders for massive inflation on everything but paychecks since before I started my professional career.

The only incident the MGA had on the track was that in strong left corners, like the decreasing radius corkscrew right before the finish line, all the fuel would rush to the right side of the tank and up the fuel spout. Tech came over and warned me I'd need to get that sealed up for the next race. Funny thing is, I had this same problem on the MGB when I raced it (solved by sticking a shirt in the spout).

My most significant incidents actually came on the way home. On a strong uphill my diaper must have leaked onto the exhaust behind it and suddenly it looked like I was trying to lose someone in an old spy movie by deploying my smoke screen. Then at the gas station the attendant (Oregon requires they pump your gas) banged the handle off my taillight and broke it. He didn't offer to pay for it, and typically I'd have been jumping all over asking to see his manager but... I'm trying to work on having some grace. The taillight lens is about $10 bucks if I remember right and I know many times I've been given much more grace.

I had a great time autocrossing and TSD rallying in the last week. I may limit it to one event per weekend in the future. Even as I write this I'm still somewhat tired. I'm really looking forward to the next autocross I get to participate in. It's an addicting sport.

Can the automobile be considered art? The art community claims foul because a car has practical application, therefor barring it from any true claims of being "art". Apparently true art can have no practical application... which seems to be a life approach often adopted by artists as well. Yet throughout the summer car shows draw large crowds of uneducated masses and when the local art museum hosted an exhibition entitled "the art of car" they saw some of the largest crowds they've ever seen. So can the car be considered art? If art is simply design created to illicit emotional response, then the answer is undoubtedly yes. But if art truly isn't functional, can a car still qualify?

As a whole, in the vast majority of instances, barring some prototypes and concept cars, most cars do serve the function of people mover.

But let's take a look at the elements of a car. I think we'll find that not all are practical, and if the car as a whole can't be considered "true art", there are at least parts of the car that may qualify.

First, let's consider the basic shape. One of the key design elements is the shape. If a designed shape wasn't placed over the mechanicals, we'd all drive cars that would l the MGA.

Now we're used to car shapes that are designed to for efficiency. That wasn't always the case. There was a time when cars were designed mainly for aesthetics, with air flow efficiency a distant second thought. A famous example is the Shelby/AC Cobra. The original AC, on which the Shelby Cobra body was based, was designed to the aesthetic preferences of 1950's England. The Shelby racing team found it was horrible aerodynamically and if they were to have any chance of beating the Ferrari's on the circuits with longer straights, such as the Le Mans circuit, they'd need a new body.

 The Shelby Daytona was born, which incorporated the Cobra's underpinnings but was designed to beat the wind resistance and give Shelby's more speed on long straights. Now if the original Cobra/AC wasn't designed to be aerodynamic, wouldn't that mean the body was simply designed to be aesthetically pleasing, therefore making it a study in art?

Often designers add body style design that serves no functional purpose other than to add the designer's personal flair. One might say, it's the designer's "artistic flair" coming through. A famous example is the "double bubble" design associated with many Zagato designs. Specials from Fiats to Aston Martins wore the double humps.

Another great styling example that can only be considered art, is that Lamborghini incorporated their logo, the bull, into the shape of their Muira car. When

you open the doors, the face and horns of a bull is
clearly seen.

As previously mentioned, one might argue concept cars
could fall into the same consideration as art because
they are often designed to be looked at, with little to no
drive-ability. Their designed function is to be
aesthetically pleasing at motor shows, not to be a
people carrier.

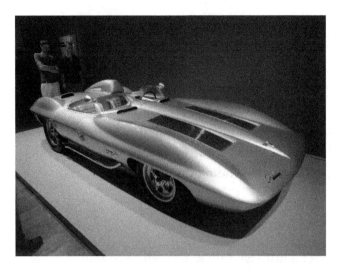

In addition to concept cars, hardcore customizers have been designing cars that were mainly for aesthetics since the turn of the century. A great example is the Brooke Swan Car from India. The only thing that disqualifies the swan on the car from being "true" art, is that the beak of the swan was designed to blow steam on dirty peasants that dared to block its path. The car caused such havoc it was barred from the road. Don't we all occasionally want a steam gun mounted to the front of our car for those "peasants"?

Almost as crazy were the creations of Ed "Big Daddy" Roth in the 60s. Beyond his famous rat fink models he created real cars as well, almost equally as bizarre.

An interesting note, Ed Roth fell away from the car scene when he joined the Hell's Angels. He hated his experience and quit. The Hell's Angels sent thugs to beat on him not realizing he was a black belt. The Angels were beat upon but they say Ed Roth lived in fear of the Angels from that time on and his art lacked its fun almost childish vibe from that point forward. The Hell's Angels have been and continue to be bad news. Don't buy into their toy drives, that's not what they represent. The last thing on earth you should do is desire to emulate them.

Anyway, again, back to cars.

Customizing like Ed Roth isn't dead though. My wife and I were recently at Moon Speed Shop in L.A. where we saw all sorts of interesting creations!

And while we're looking at the exterior of cars, let's discuss paint jobs. Now paint does have the function of covering the metal to prevent rust, so let's consider base coats functional. The embellishments laid over that base paint should be considered expressions in art because they no longer function as rust inhibitors.

A great example is the famous, and now 60 years later much overdone, flame job affectionately dubbed "crab claws". When first invented, they were a cool expression in art and they can still look great on the right car.

Another great example, originally popularized in the 1950s, is pinstriping. Von Dutch was the most famous pinstriper, applying his marks to many classic hot rods. How the name Von Dutch moved from an association to pinstriping to an association with a brand rich kids wear is utterly beyond me.

Even Andy Warhol got into embellishing cars painting a BMW M1. And let's not forget the Janis Joplin "art car" that just sold at auction for boo-khoo bucks.

And just as art can be considered poor quality, the same can be said of the embellishments placed on cars. Consider the bizarre paint job on my 1990s commuter car. The only way those embellishment could be considered displayable art is if a thousand years passes and someone digs the side panel up and decides to display them on their wall as ancient artifacts.

Let's move past paint embellishments though and talk about chrome and emblems. Chrome and emblems are art because they serve no purpose other than to increase the visual aesthetics of a car.

First let's consider one of the most iconic emblems of all time, the prancing horse of Ferrari. A WW1 Italian ace's family crest that he painted on the side of his planes for luck. He died and his family later asked Mr. Ferrari to place the symbol as good luck on his racing cars (interestingly at that time he was actually managing Alfa's racing team and the prancing horse can be found on some early Alfas). Perhaps a bad omen of things to come, because for a period of time Ferrari was famous for losing racing drivers in accidents. But regardless, the prancing horse has become one of the most iconic automotive industry emblems.

Or if you're more into American cars, how about the iconic chrome embellishments of the 1950's Chevys? These pieces of chrome instantly bring to mind golden visions of milk shakes, drive-ins, hot rods, rock and roll, etc. If a single piece of embellishment can cause such emotive response, how can it not be considered art?

Two of the most iconic cars have two pointless embellishments. Both the 1957 Chevy Bel Air and the 1965 Mustang had the option of hubcaps that resemble knock-off wheel assemblies. These hubcaps served no purpose although designed to look like a center wheel lock. To this day, hubcaps are still used as aesthetic embellishment's, sometimes with disastrously distasteful results. If you can buy it at Auto Zone or WalMart, the chances are it's in poor taste. Should you find yourself in front of a car shaped like a swan, be prepared for a steam bath.

The chrome from the 1950's also reflected a culture that was just entering the space age with great anticipation. Jets and Rockets were commonly incorporated into automotive design during the 1950's.

Some of these chrome ornaments even chance into the art designation of statue. Consider the famous Spirit of Ecstasy or The Archer. Both magnificent statue miniatures that graced the hood of early 20th century cars.

The luxury cars that these early hood emblems adorned often incorporated a lot of chrome, beautiful shape, and other artistic touches that make these cars magnificent to look upon.

If you opened the door you'd see other examples of embellishment without function. Take for example doors skinned with ostrich skin as found in the Bugatti Atlantic.

Even under the hood one can find examples of embellishment without function. For example, valve covers often incorporate artistic touches.

So I make the case that although car may have the purpose of being functional, many of its design elements can include truly artistic touches. As those pieces are incorporated into what the car becomes as a sum of the whole, the car itself may become an element of art.

The chances are that if you read to this point, you already agreed with me, but if you really were considering this pointless theological topic I urge you to consider the automobile as art if it incorporates some of the elements discussed above in a tasteful way.

Rallycross!

Today I had a great time rallycrossin! If you haven't done rallycross I'd highly recommend it. What a blast!

I also tried to hit up the local MGA clubs monthly meeting - http://www.columbiagorgemgaclub.org/ Somehow I got the time wrong and ended up walking in at 730 to see a sign on the door saying MGA club meeting at 630. I decided to pass on being an hour late my first time so I'll have to tell you how that club is some other time.

I'd been looking forward to rallycross ever since I'd heard about it from some guys at the time-speed-distance rally. It was explained to me that rallycross is simply autocross on dirt.

I'd seen pictures of rallycross at other venues and it looked idyllic with classics traipsing over green pastures.

Then I heard our local rallycross was held at a rock quarry which made me less excited.

At the next time-speed-distance rally the same guys assured me though, it was simply right next to the rock quarry. When you really think about it, that logic makes little sense when you're considering the amount of rocks, but thankfully I didn't really think about it.

When we got out there today we discovered that the race is held in a sunken area that I can only imagine was the rock quarry at some point before it moved slightly to the south. The dirt is rock hard and rutted, which is consistent with a site that's seen a lot of heavy equipment move across it.

The all-wheel drives (AWD) run in the morning and watching them didn't make me excited to run. The site was REALLY dusty, and rutted. But I steeled my resolved, reminding myself that there's not a whole lot in the MGA that can get dirty right now (no insulation or carpet) and that, short of coupe door parts, there's nothing I can break that will cost an exorbitant amount to replace. One of the blessings of MGA ownership is that parts are plentiful.

Walking the track before our run time we came across several rocks the AWDs had kicked up which were at least a foot long and 5 inches tall. One of the guys was talking about how, in order to make his car ready for this particular site, he's put a skid plate on the bottom of the car. The rock and the comment made me start visualizing my oil pan gushing oil after striking a similar rock.

Then we headed for the start line. Earlier I watched another guy's windshield get pelted with rocks and I learned not to wait directly behind the car starting, especially if it's rear wheel drive.

I somehow ended up at the front of the line and while they sorted the timing machine I got a nice pause with all sorts of thoughts running through my head like, "should I really be doing this?"

Then I got the green light, or wave out is more realistic.

Then it all kicked back in. Suddenly I was 16 years old pitching my truck across the desert again. Two inches of dust powder in an MGA is a lot like a truck on the desert roads I learned to drive on.

I was having a blast. There's something awesome about turning into a corner 10 feet before and steering with your throttle.

The freshly adjusted carbs let second gear rev up to around 4k comfortably. There were two longer sections where I could use another gear but the ratios between 2nd and 3rd are just too far apart and I found myself bogging when I dropped into 3rd gear. My last two or three runs I didn't use third at all.

The dust was atrocious but I was having so much fun I didn't care. I've posted this video so you can get an idea of how dusty it was but you can't see me for too much of it, the course was too spread out.

https://www.youtube.com/watch?v=akcBy_8yO_0

You're supposed to run the event with your windows up but my freshly greased window channels kept letting the driver's window come down with each big bump. At one point, a competitor going through a corner next to me sent a wave of dust through my window which hit me in the face even through the helmet and glasses. I imagine the Baja 1000 guys are picking sand out of crazy places for months with all the dust that race kicks up.

Eventually there was a big rock laying in the middle of the course but thankfully I managed to miss it every time (I think).

The MGA took the course like a champ, the lever action shocks sucking the bumps up surprisingly well. There was one bump though that kept kicking the MGA airborne that wasn't very comfortable. Not sure any suspension short of an expensive one could deal with that bump.

After each run I listened for strange ticks, worriedly checked the oil and temp gauge, and walked around the car looking for problems. I couldn't find any problems though. As far as I can tell, no damage was done. Not bad considering, in total, I was driving it all out for about 7.5 minutes on a very bumpy rocky dirt road. I've broke trucks faster than that.

I want to be sure and mention my wife braved the dust, even 4.5 months pregnant, to take these great pictures!

I did have the same problem as the autocross though, I'm having a hard time keeping the tire with power on the ground. I need to fit an MGB sway bar before my next competition. I had my fastest time not when I focused on going as "all out" as I could, but when I focused on keeping traction and modulating my throttle a little more judiciously.

I took first in the stock rear-wheel drive class. I was the only rear wheel drive stock car. I'm hoping we forget that with time.

I've got a trophy in the garage for "best Asian motorcycle" that I won under similar circumstances. I'd restored a 1969 Honda S-90 and taken it to a pre-1970 car and bike show. Turns out, there wasn't many Asian bikes from before 1970 and I was the only one there.

In a way I'm proud of my, "I'm the only one doing this" trophies because they represent that I don't always do things the same as other people do. In a world that I think is flat out crazy mostly, I'm proud to know that I'm consistently different.

After the races I spit the dirt out of my mouth and it looked like mud because I'd inhaled so much dust. We were due at a friend's going away party and my wife wasn't quite sure how we (mainly I) was going to recover without going home because I was so filthy. Plus the car had a nice layer of dust coating it. Well, I hope the janitor at Kmart doesn't hate me, I tried to clean that bathroom up as best I could.

When I got home I spent quite a bit of time with the vacuum, Windex and hose cleaning the car up. The neighbors probably think I'm crazy for "washing" such an ugly car! The hoods up in the pic because I started the motor and washed it down too.

Now here's the question - Would I do it again?

The organizer told me that they forgot to schedule the water truck in time. I might make sure the water truck was there before heading out again, but..., because my car is empty right now, it didn't take much longer than an hour to clean tonight. It's the same as if I'd went out motorcycle riding all day.

The track had to have been hard on the car. Most the other cars out there were modified beaters. I wish I could build an MGB beater just for rallycross but my wife says "No more cars, four is enough for two people". I suppose she's right.

In the end, I'll probably hold out for the rallycross that looks more like the idyllic pictures of rolling greens with cars racing across them. But then the little voice in the back of my head says, "Stop being a pansy and use that MGA hard".

What I'd really like to do is to talk a friend into buying a car for it. Then it wouldn't be at my house. If you're my friend, and you're reading this, I think you should buy a car! It's a blast! One of the fastest cars out there today was a stripped 280z. Those aren't too expensive, do it! You'll love it.

Cars and Coffee

It was 2013 when I discovered Cars and Coffee, and I'm a big fan. What could be better than:

Staggering out of bed an hour later than weekdays,

Not shaving or brushing your teeth,

Wearing your ugly grease stained car themed t-shirt you love,

Putting your chores off for at least 2 hours,

Stumbling to the car to drive to a car show at 8 a.m,

Which is conveniently in front of a coffee shop where you can grab a black coffee and a pastry,

Watching the sun come up over the hill on a convertible Stingray,

and talkin' cars with other nuts just like you?!

Some fine cars show up too. For example, I don't think I'd ever seen a vintage limo Bentley in the flesh before. Wow, they really are a special car. There's a presence of grandeur when you see them in person. It's as if the castle should be tagging behind shortly. Makes you want to refer to funny things like the "bonnet" and consider drinking tea instead (but only very briefly).

There's also some odd cars. For example, the Lotus Europa is so ugly that I can't help but love it. It looks like a great looking sports car and a little Toyota pickup had a baby together.

You'll also find the American car show classics as well. Yes, you've seen 5,000 versions of the same car, starting with the three your dad owned when you were a kid, but there are Chevelles, Corvettes, Camaros, Mustangs, etc. etc. etc.. And yes, I'd still own number 5001 in a heartbeat if I could afford one. Thanks dad, for destruction derbying your big block Challenger because "it was ugly". Ok, I understand that; the later

Challengers were ugly, even if people are paying too much for them 20 years later.

Also, the funky cars make an appearance. Cars that when you talk to the owner they mention things like their inability to keep the rear axle together if they actually use the power plant they put in the car. Oops. Some people need a poster in their garage that reminds them, "you're only as strong as your weakest link". But I still admire these people. They are the brave... and generally poor. I guess I'd like to imagine I can relate, but perhaps I'm not brave. My 1957 MGA has a big 72 horsepower in top shape.

Note that these guys are proud of their motors. Yes, they did something disgusting... disgustingly awesome. And they're proud of it. Therefore the hood pops open. And guys like me love it! Don't forget, there are two parts of the car, form and function! This is one of my suggestions to make cars and coffee a little better. Even if you have no idea how that noisy thing under the hood works, open the hood up for those of us that do.

But let's get back to who attend, we can't forget the ridiculously expensive cars. And these people don't play around. Life is a competition. "What...", someone else brought a V12 supercar? Park right next to them so you can prove your superiority. Ferrari or McLaren? A question I'll never have the authority to answer. It's like that goofy kid that drives the Geo Metro but wears a

Ferrari jacket - he has no real authority to tell the world that Ferrari is so worthy but he'll wear their name on his chest 300 days a year.

I think the McLaren looks better. Seriously Ferrari, hoop roll bars? What is this, a BMW Z3? McLaren's shaped buttresses harken back to the days of 1950's sports car racing; dig it!

My first couple of Cars and Coffee I took very few photos and enjoyed the coffee, cars, and people. Then this blog started to get more popular. What does that have to do with the price of tea in china?

I started getting death threats from photographers whose posted internet pictures I was copying and pasting into my blog. Some creepy lawyer-esque guy sent me a two page blog response on legal precedence regarding using photos, even if they're posted on the internet for all the world to see.

I then realized that if I didn't want to have to deal with these types, I needed to have a stock of my own photos that covered all the types of cars I might have an itching to write about.

Today I took more photos to hold in my back pocket. Here's a few of the highlights. And I give anyone permission to use the photos in this blog anyway they want. I won't sue you even if I see my photos printed individually on each toilet paper square. Who knows, it might sell! People really could say, "I wipe my butt with (insert hated car marque here)".

A nice 1960s V12 Ferrari was in attendance this morning.

But I hate to say it, I found myself thinking the unthinkable. Pinafarina's influence is so clear that I could see a little bit of MGB in the body lines!

And my photo shooting skills are lacking. I had to "antique" this photo because it was the only way the lack of focus made any sense. Fail at having a vintage Ferrari V12 photo in my stock. From the other side I got an excellent photo (sarcasm) focused on the battery post, while behind it you can barely make out a blurry Ferrari valve cover.

And I can't forget the random angle photos I shot trying to be artistic. Too bad there's a 240Z tattooed on the leather seat and my pants are displayed prominently in the mirror.

But I did get away with a Ferrari emblem. And it's MY PHOTO. Bwa ha ha ha. I can use it without anyone suing me. Old man Ferrari probably could/would but he's dead. Ain't it pretty? And don't forget the bling; chrome!

I thought a Porsche logo might come in handy someday too. The owner told me this is a very rare factory 911 paint color on this 914. It's green. Slight sarcasm, but I will admit it was a great color for the car.

Speaking of Porsche, I don't normally like them but this one looked great. The color, the mirror, the bumpers, the brass cooler lines, the moderately flared fenders... I'd drive it. Even if my own family would make tons of yuppie jokes. Working in a city, owning a 911, and having country relatives is a recipe for ridicule.

A couple of stalls away I happened upon a vintage right hand drive Porsche that I wanted to know more about. I couldn't find the owner, but I give him props for leaving the windows open so I could check out the interior without glare. This is another thing I'd recommend for all attendees. Hoods up, windows down!

Here's another fail shot at being artistic. Quite the snout on that Porsche huh?

The unimog had a Michelin man mounted on its rear view mirror. You probably get him for free when you buy a set of tires for this truck!

If I've seen 5,000 of everything else American, I've probably seen 20,000 Mustangs. But I still love the fastback. Hence this shot of only the fastback. I'm tired of the rest of the car.

Now imagine a classic beautiful 1960's Lancia. Then imagine if they partnered with Zagato. Remember the magic of the Aston Zagato. Here's what Lancia achieved with Zagato. I wonder if Lancia asked for their money back?

I was very impressed with a classic BMW's interior. Looked great! I can imagine he loves to drive it. The exterior of the car... kinda cool. The interior... if I owned it I might sleep in it; excellent!

Well, I hope you enjoyed some of the fruits of my attempt at avoiding litigation. Make sure you check out a Cars and Coffee. And when you're there, and you see the goofy guy taking photos of every little thing with a crappy $200 dollar camera, make sure you say "hi" to me. Don't worry, I'll tell you whether I think the Ferrari or McLaren is better even if you don't care about my opinion because you saw me show up in my Geo Metro (it's just my commuter!).

My Top Six

What are the six best and worst looking classic cars in the world? Is there a question that could possibly be more based on personal taste and nation of upbringing? Well, here I am weighing in with my highly esteemed opinion. I'm sure this piece will instantly affect auction values. I do imagine this is the most controversial concept in cars.

#6 Best Looking Car in the World - Mercedes 500

A beautiful stately car. Images of German castles seem to pop into mind just by looking at the car. The flowing body lines put the car into perpetually graceful motion. And for those of us that are a little simpler, there's a lot of shiny chrome. "Oooo.... shiny!"

#6 Worst Looking Car in the World - Mercedes 500

Why yes, that is Adolf Hitler next to his car of choice, the ominous black Mercedes 500. I'm throwing a kicker at you but based on this car's historical relevance as Hitler's parade car I'd say it's equally as ugly as it is beautiful. One could argue it's a perfect time piece for its generation. Nations banded together in a fight for good and evil to a scale possibly never seen before and in that you'll find some of the greatest stories of mankind as well as some of the worst. The Mercedes too shows how grand man's creation can be, but it also speaks volumes to the depths of evil man will fall in their pursuit of grandeur. And it's just a car.

And as a side note, there is nothing uglier than an 80's Excalibur replica of the classic Mercedes; it's a pitiful attempt at recreating a world class car. Much like an awkward youth trying to wear the clothes of a famous star in an effort to recreate their "look", it's just not the same.

#5 Worst Looking Car in the World - US Spec Rubber Bumper MGB

This one hits close to home because I used to own the one pictured. But that's also why I hate the late MGBs. U.S. safety rules had required that the front springs be extended to increase the front bumper height drastically affecting the stance. The chrome bumpers were removed for "safer" rubber bumpers that looked hideous. Giant marker lights were added to the side of the body breaking up the clean lines. The leather and metal interior in the early 60's MGBs was replaced with plastic and vinyl. A 3rd windshield wiper was added to the windshield to meet US spec wiper coverage laws.

In 20 years MG had made a progressively worse car, which was mirrored across British Leyland. Not only is this car ugly but it represents a national sports car industry crumbling!

#5 Best Looking Car in the World – Duesenberg Cars

What can be said? Just look at it! It's magnificent. From every angle it's just a little prettier, smoother and cleaner than the Mercedes. The choice of the rich and famous!

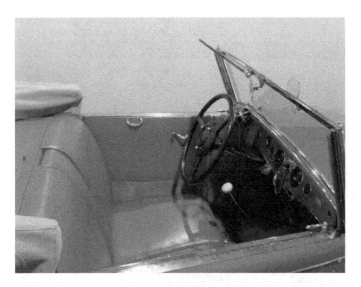

And it wasn't just pretty, it was also fast! It's like its saying, "I'm good looking but I'm also strong and will beat on you a little if you try and mess with me".

#4 Worst

They're just not pretty. That wasn't their point. They were to be the cars for the masses designed by a despot. They eventually were called the beetle/bug and a more appropriate name couldn't be found. They look like a stink bug puckering up its rear end getting ready for an expulsion of stink. And ironically, thanks to loose tolerances and low compression, often they did send stink out the tailpipe. And as they aged they only became fatter and less utilitarian.

But I'd take an early one. Its ugliness works for it. I love the oval window and flip up traffic signals that come out of the door to signal for turns.

#4 Best Looking Car in the World - 1957 Chevy Bel Air

It's as American as a cheeseburger or Ronald Reagan. It's iconic and represents a generation that came before the cultural revolution of the 60's and 70's. There's never been a better looking piece of chrome than its side panel. It could be made into a hot rod with relative ease, and pictures of youth surrounding it at drive-ins came to represent an entire decade. And it looks good stock or as a custom. It is the pen-ultimate 1950's design. I may buy a reproduction of the chrome just to hang on my garage wall. The 1957 Chevy Bel Air is American car culture at its best.

I felt like I couldn't even talk about the Bel Air without inserting a picture of a drive-in.

#3 Worst Looking Car in the World - 1969-72 Mustang

Like the MGB and the Bug, the Mustang got a few years under its belt and gained weight. Hey, quite a few of us have been there so it's hard to hold just that against it but it didn't gain weight gracefully. It didn't gain weight proportionally. Look at the photos. The motor area is the same size as the original motor but the cabin and rear end are huge! Basically, its rear end got awkwardly large. That aint good!

And on top of that, Ford and/or the owners began embellishing them with all sorts of cheap plasticky bits. Why would anyone want louvres on their rear window, cowl induction that faces the wrong way, or spoilers that provide little to no downward force.

And as the years went by it only got worse. It barely even resembled a mustang by the mid-70s. Too much plastic surgery can be disastrous if done without regard to taste.

#3 Best Looking Car in the World - Shelby Daytona

This car was built with a purpose - it had to be aerodynamic enough to beat the Ferraris. Yet as often happens when something is built with aesthetic abandonment while working towards a strictly functional goal of epic proportion, the end result is gorgeous. There isn't a car in the world, to this day, that looks better screaming around a track. And beat the Ferrari team it did. It's easy to love a winner, and when it's the Daytona Coupe it becomes one of the best looking cars in the world.

#2 Worst Looking Car in the World - The (Two Word) Sting Ray Corvette

Yes, the Corvette was always plastic (made out of fiberglass and resin) but it's as though Chevy decided to highlight it. In 1970 they came out with a Corvette that looked so plastic that cheap is the only word that can be used to describe it. None of the curves work for it. The rear end looked terrible. The snout looked too long. And it's sort of a targa?! Couple appalling looks with one of the heaviest most underpowered American motors ever produced and you have one of the ugliest cars ever made.

I don't even have a photo of one. I've never felt the urge to pull the camera's trigger.

#2 Best Looking Car in the World - Any Bentley from 1925-1931

How many of you read the Wind in the Willows as a child? In the story there's a rich toad who lives in Toad Manor, who has few socially redeeming qualities and is madly in love with the automobile to the extent he disregards all his friends in pursuit of his hobby. And the car that's parked in front of Toad Manor, as imagined by almost every young boy, is an iconic Bentley produced in the late 1920's.

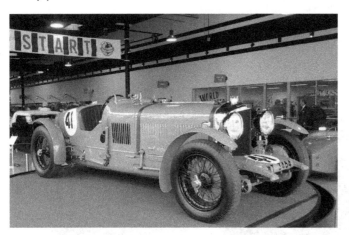

These Bentley's are the ultimate British sports car. Everything else in the period was simply trying to be a Bentley. They are not swoopy or aerodynamic per se, but what they lack in grace they make up in brute strength. Combine that British Resolve with British Racing Green paint and you have one of the most iconic and best looking cars ever made.

#1 Worst Looking Car in the World - Citroen DS

It's so bizarre it's cool. Only the French could come up with it. It bears no resemblance to anything, and in no way hints at any strength. It is an amorphous blog that moves down the road floating on air. It would look perfect parked in front of a French bakery picking up pastries. It is a pastry of a car. Round, soft, bulging.

Open the door and you'll see that the car is also somewhat bulimic. It appears to be throwing up its steering wheel.

I can't think of any uglier car, but it's so ugly and awkward it's awesome.

#1 Best Looking Car in the World – Any pre-1965 Ferrari

Yes, as record sale prices reach tens of million dollars, I end with a safe choice. But even if they were as cheap as an early MGB, I'd still love the Ferrari. It screams 1950s/60s racer but with an extremely dignified split personality. This car looks as good tearing up a track as it does sitting on the golf course at the Pebble Beach Concourse d'Elegance.

And it looks amazing in Rosso Corsa (Ferrari's red of choice).

There you have it, my opinion. Not worth much is it? I haven't driven any of them and for all you know I could be writing this in my mom's basement, eating Cheetos, never having earned my driver's license. Rest assured, I'm sure you'll take my picks into consideration for your next purchase.

Now is the Winter of my Discontent

It snowed close to 8 inches in Portland Oregon last week and that night it took me 3 hours to drive the 25 miles to my home. As I sat in my Geo Metro, crawling past Jeeps, 4Runners and Durango's who'd somehow managed to drive into the ditch at 5 mph, I couldn't help but think the snowy traffic jam aligned with how my car project is going. It's a cold, grey, bleak, dreary, February, and I'm stuck waiting on the motor shop and March's budget dollars... now is the winter of my classic car discontent.

Thought I'd share a picture I snapped of a really fancy BMW M series XB stuck in traffic next to me. A thought struck me then - same commute, same piece of road, same situation, and he's out $100k(?) grand more than me. I bet he had grand delusions of blasting through the snow in his high performance SUV when he bought it. Traffic that day was the winter of his discontent too. You can tell in the picture by the way he's driving outside where everyone else was to test his off-road capability. He may have been trying to get in my lane but... fancy big expensive BMW not using his blinker... yeah... not going to give space for that lane change. Me and the Metro fighting The Man.

So, what can you do while you wait for spring? Well, when I picked up my pistons I went out to the British car shop. Stan, the Saturday shop keeper, told me I could wander around the garage. I wish I hadn't. I found myself under an MGA whose axle you could eat off because it was so clean; the running gear was like new. That made me green with envy and now I'm going to attempt the same feat. What a waste of time in a car that leaked from the factory.

That meant another date with the wire wheel to get the 50 years of rust off of my exhaust. I hope inhaling rust particles doesn't kill brain or lung cells. And hopefully the exhaust wasn't galvanized under that rust because I hear that will kill cells. But I also hear almost anything kills brain cells. Glass of wine - kills brain cells. Fart and smell it - kills brain cells. Being voted into public office - kills brain cells. Etc. etc. etc.

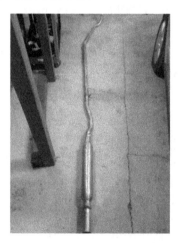

Once the exhaust was cleaned I realized I had no idea how to keep it from rusting back up.

I then wheeled the frame out to give the rear end a good scrub down. 60 years of British gunk slowly pealed away with a screwdriver and electrical cleaner. Yeah, I thought buying the pressure washer eliminated my need to do that but it just doesn't have enough oomph to deal with British grease. As archaic as this car is, with its starting handle, the grease is probably made of Sperm Whale blubber.

After the rear end's grease protective layer was pealed away I could finally read the axle gear ratio. Unfortunately it's the same ratio as the wire wheel rear end I have in the shed so I won't gain any speed if I switch over to wires. Another argument for leavin' the steel wheels on there.

 At some point in here I stopped by my work's garage. What a setup! Each bench has a crane. I could have used that when I was pushing my motor up my motorcycle ramp to get it on my workbench!

Weeknights and weekends I've found myself cleaning and painting. Sway bars, fan pulleys, oil pans, you name it, I'm cleaning it.

I've made a pretty good dent on the to-do list. Essentially everything in the parts pile but my horn is either ready for paint or painted.

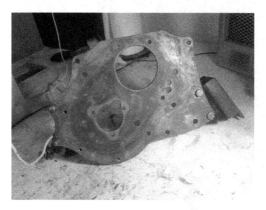

We took a short trip to nearby McMinnville to get out of the house. I found this old Locomobile parked in a bank lobby with a plaque stating it was the first car to make it over the mountains West of Portland and down to Tillamook (where the good cheese comes from).

 With a little online research I found that the driver wrote a book about the trip called "A Horseless Carriage Comes to Town" in 1966. I found an autographed copy on amazon for $13 dollars. I'm looking forward to reading it.

And I'm looking forward to getting my motor back! And March's budget. It feels good to be almost to the "putting things back together" phase. I just wish it was here already. I'm tired of February.

10 Ugly Classic Cars, and Why We Think They Look Awesome Regardless

Some classic cars were designed for a trendsetter that lived in a place where the locals are beautiful, but others were designed by an individual named Bruno who lived in a place where the locals have taken their share of beatings from the ugly stick. Yet somehow Bruno has managed to design classic cars that still manage to look "good" despite the brutality of their design. You'd never say Bruno's cars are gorgeous; a classic red Ferrari his cars are not. But they capture your eye and heart just the same.

There's a place in the world for Bruno's cars. If you handed the keys to a red Ferrari to the local iron yard riveter he would likely steal it and sell it for beer money and hunting supplies. He wouldn't keep the red Ferrari because he'd be ashamed to be seen in such a girly-man car. He doesn't like Italian designer jeans, cologne, etc. and he thinks you have to in order to drive a Ferrari.

But if you hand the riveter the keys to Bruno's creation he'll wear t-shirts emblazoned with the car manufacturer's logo every weekend for the rest of his life. He may still steal the car, but he'll park it on his lawn when he gets home and then sit in a lawn chair drinking whiskey while staring at it because he's suffering from an overwhelming man crush. His girlfriend will leave him for Earl in the trailer down the "court" because all he'll ever talk about is the car and soon his only friends will be other gentleman of similar distinction (typically found at car shows highlighting the car's manufacturer).

What are these cars? I've made a top 10 list based on my experience and taste. The first five on the list don't have the engine displacement and ferocity to appeal to a steel riveter. These are cars owned by guys that just can't see themselves in a "pretty" car, but their testosterone production isn't quite what it may have been. They'll take ugly and slower, a surprising pick for sure, but a comfortable place for them. Sound harsh? Don't worry, the author may self-identify with this group.

Don't agree with my conclusions? Well good, put the beer can down and write your snarky remarks in an email to the author letting me know why you and your car show buddies think that the car I named isn't ugly.

#10

The (original) Fiat Abarth – Seriously, you have to prop the motor cover open just to fit the parts in? And did Fiat pay someone to design a body that looks like two squares welded together? And don't forget, if you truly want to cool that hot motor, you'll have to plumb cooling into the front end giving it the look of a flat faced boxer with a fat lip.

#9

The Datsun 510 – They say the best looking cars are designed with the shape of a woman in mind. The 510 was designed with the body of a short stubby man in mind. But he was a strong stubby man. And the 510 proved that although it was the short kid on the block it still packed a wallup.

#8

The Volvo P1800 – This is the car shape you get when designed by people that have to survive a harsh winter climate but still allow themselves the fancy of believing in elves, gnomes and fairies. Up front the car has a strong motor fronted with a somewhat awkward grille and surrounded by good looking fenders, but the body tapers back to strange frivolous fins.

#7

The Saab 96 – this car was produced in a town called Trollhattan. No surprise then that a troll would feel perfectly at home behind the wheel. No other classic car could ferry him between the snowy bridges he frequents with the speed and anger he requires.

#6

The Jensen CV – In black they look best (which in itself says something about a car) but their lines don't quite flow, they have odd headlights, and the front end would probably best be described as a snout. Yet somehow they still look good. I've never been to Ireland, but I imagine that for a manager working the Irish shipyards if the laborers spotted you driving the CV you wouldn't have to fear any ridicule; you have to maintain whatever fleeting perception of authority you have when pressing the union workforce for production.

#5

Allard Cars – One can only hope that Mr. Allard made a conscious decision to simply wrap his American motored V8 rockets in sheet metal as a necessity, rather than style the body. Based on looks it appears the

Allard is the epitome of function before form. For example, yes it has a radiator grille. The purpose of the Allard grille is to provide airflow to the radiator while blocking the birds from going through the radiator, The Allard grille is not meant to look good. Almost every visible part on the Allard can be summarized in similar fashion.

#4

The Big Block Cobras – As the power and ferocity grew inside the quant little British designed body strange bulges and protrusions also grew around the exterior of the car. Like a steroid induced body builder, the big Cobras don't look natural in their own skin. You almost expect them to tear their hood off at any minute like a flashback to 1980's steroid lovin' Hulk Hogan ripping his shirts in half before wrestling matches.

#3

The AMC Javelin in Trans Am guise – an underdog always looks good whipping on the pretty boys. And in 1970 the Javelin did just that, giving the Mustangs and Camaros a one-two punch on the Trans Am circuit. But the Javelin was not pretty. In fact, it was really ugly. Why? Likely it was heralding in the decade. It seems most designers agreed "It's 1970 and a new decade, let's try ugly from here on out".

#2

The Lamborghini Countach – Even its name in Italian is vulgar (google it if you don't believe me). But it was awesome. Ugly in a way only Italy could do – ugly beautiful. It was utter rebellion. Compare the sloping curvaceous lines of the 1960's Ferraris with this upstart from just a few years later. Everything was different. It was big. It was angular. It was impractical. It was mean. But yet, somehow still Italian. And when you think Italian sports car, you just can't think of barrel chested men driving them. Had the car been made in America I'm certain it would have made number one on this list. It would have made sense. It's a brutal, ugly, hard to drive car with impressive power. But Italy is the land of playboys and somehow you can't escape the sense that the only person driving the Countach is a man that goes to the tanning bed, wears a v-neck shirt with a sport jacket, and protects his eyes with oversized designer sunglasses. Pity the Countach, it can't escape its origins.

#1

And the winner is a twofer – The Charger and Barracuda of the 60s. Dyno tests now tell us that Dodge was lying about the horsepower of these Hemi monstrosities by underrating them severely, when the competition was doing the opposite to compete. These cars are brutally powerful and they look like a drug fueled biker club member would be comfortable driving them. The large body and wide grille can be compared with a fist coming at you fast with a large powerful forearm behind it. There's a reason the bad guy drove a black charger in Bullet. Have you ever seen a white Charger? The

Charger and Barracuda epitomize tough. Don't believe me? I dare you to kick the next guy you see wearing a Mopar shirt in the shins.

Go-Karts and Soapbox Derby Racing, or Some Things Never Change

Twice in a week I've been able to partake in some classic motorsport, although no one calls it that. For both sports the roots go back over 100 years. And in both cases everyone involved was having a blast and I walked away with a smile on my face. But unlike vintage Ferrari racing, which you won't touch for under $100k, these were events shared with the "unwashed masses" (probably why I was there). Let's talk about some vintage racing you can enjoy for pennies, if it's a big jar.

On Monday, my buddy Andrew and I headed over to the local indoor go-kart racing track, Sykart, for their endurance race night. On endurance race night, for $30 you get 30 minutes of racing in one shot.

For a half hour 9 karts battled around the track. We bumped more than the track manager would have preferred and we got warned. We slid through corners as we tried to figure out apexes. We brushed up against walls and even bounced off them when we exited corners too high. We tried to cut off the one guy driving the "special membership" kart repeatedly. And we got out of the karts laughing, adrenalin pumping, talking in that loud obnoxious guy voice (that society has told us we are supposed to kill for a life of office work and emasculation), making fighter jet pilot gestures with our hands as we talked about our superior performances. The printed lap time sheets told us 12 year old girls were faster earlier in the day but we ignored that.

It was a total blast. I can't recommend it more. As always, I wish it was even cheaper, but it's hard to argue with $30 dollars. If it was $15 I'd be there every Monday night!

Tonight, as I write this, the riots in Ferguson continue and I can't help but thinking more people should go kart racing and get some of that energy out.

In racing, you're wearing a helmet and gloves, so racism is impossible. When you're done and leaving the track it seems as if you're all in the same club, even if it's a go-kart race. Of course that's a silly concept, only the love of Christ truly defeats hatred in the end, but God created us with the ability to have fun and we might as well enjoy it. And doing fun things more than one culture can enjoy ain't going to hurt anything. I don't think...let's say yodeling, will ever have the same cross-cultural appeal.

Watching the (so called) History channel, when Rick Dale and his team on American Restorations restored an old 1960's McCulloch go-kart (Season 2, Episode 12) they told us it was one of the earliest go-karts made. In typical History Channel fashion this seems to be an exaggeration for the sake of drama. At the following link witness a girl circa 1935 riding on an electric go-kart.

http://www.gettyimages.com/detail/news-photo/girl-smiles-while-sitting-in-the-drivers-seat-of-an-news-photo/3226297#

The antique go-kart website tells us that the first go-kart advertisement was in 1958. I have a hard time accepting that the above kart was sold without marketing but maybe.

In researching this blog one of the more interesting karting stories I came across was Walt Disney. Did you know that in 1956, when Tomorrowland opened up, Walt Disney included a road course for young men and women to learn how to drive? Walt had a vision that this course would help prepare youth for their future driving endeavors.

As the track aged, lessons were learned, and the world got more boring, Disney put in tracks that didn't allow freedom of movement and true autonomy of the young driver. Turns out seven year olds aren't the best drivers and don't mind slamming into things; actually seven year olds love smashing into things!

A version of Autopia still exists at Disneyland to this day. Not aware of its history, I skipped it during my one visit to the park and now I'm a little bummed. Not sure why but if something is boring a little history can make it more interesting. I'm pretty sure that's how the show Pawn Stars stays on the air.

Looking back at my own life I can say that go-karting has helped inform at least one of my larger life decisions, (insert adjective) as that may be. Several of my wife Kellie and I's first dates included go-karting experiences.

I can't find the Sykart photos from our first date (yes, I'm that cool), but the below photos from Oaks Park amusement park show a big smile. For you single guys, I'd suggest that if you take a girl karting and she frowns the whole time, it's an ominous sign of an inability to have fun! There's probably something wrong with her if she can't enjoy karting. Or you forgot to tell her that you were going go-karting and she did her hair and is wearing a dress. Then it's probably your fault.

Saturday of the same week I went go-karting, I took my family and some friends to the Mt. Tabor Portland Adult Soap Box Derby. The soap box concept is the same as when you're a kid, but the karts are a little more impressive. Take for example my favorite from this year, Mr. Potato Head in a Radio Flyer below. It sure beats the monstrosity my friends and I welded together, at 12 years old, from several different motorcycles and pushed to the top of a local hill before blowing through several four way intersections (not a sanctioned event).

Before I show you too much of Portland's Derby, lets first look at the history of soap box type racers. From what I see, they seem to have been around as long as carriages. It makes sense. Little boys are going to race things with wheels. Always have, always will.

At the following link there's a photo of some boys playing in a carriage around 1850. I'd be willing to bet they pushed it down some hills or at least the mansions stairs: http://www.gettyimages.com/detail/news-photo/untitled-c1792-1850-found-in-the-collection-of-the-louvre-news-photo/463918519

One of my favorite historical soapbox derby notes is during the depression artists were put to work (through the federal Works Progress Administration) on such illustrious assignments as advertisements for soap box derbies. Your grandfathers taxes hard at work!

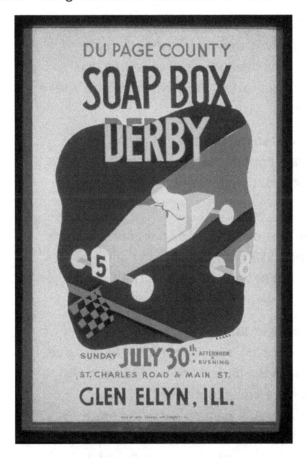

DU PAGE COUNTY
SOAP BOX
DERBY
5
8
SUNDAY JULY 30th AFTERNOON & EVENING
ST. CHARLES ROAD & MAIN ST.
GLEN ELLYN, ILL.

1939 WPA Art Project

Back to Portland in 2014. If soap box derbies remind you of the town where It's a Wonderful Life was filmed, A lot of Pottersville has snuck into Portland.   You remember Pottersville right? The evil parallel dimension where Mr. Potter had taken over the town?

In Portland in 2014, many of the contestants are so drunk you wonder how they'll make it to the bottom; and some don't. The previous year we went to the Derby the ambulance carted a team of drunks off after a spectacular crash.

And then there was some weird kart that had a giant head with a mullet booming out a recording from a 70s sci-fi film talking about phallic symbols which were all over the kart.

Possibly not the best event to take your impressionable child to, but I think at 7 months ours can't quite be influenced by these people yet. Hopefully it's not in the water.

But phallic symbol kart aside, there were some other great designs in the pits! Walking through the pits gives you a chance to see the derby karts up-close and also to judge how drunk the drivers/riders are. This is important because you'll want to watch the more hammered participants go down because 1. They may crash (and who doesn't want to see that?), and 2. You don't want to be near the track when they are crashing.

The ghosts of Lewis and Clark made an appearance. They've adapted well to modern Portland thanks to ghost beer.

The derby karts get a push start at the top.

The first hill is a little slow but it's a good spot for spectators.

Mt Tabor itself is a good sized hill and they've got lots of time to come up to speed!

And by the bottom they're flat out booking it.

So there it is. Two ways you can have a blast racing without having the last name Vanderbilt. You can even call it vintage racing if its makes you feel more special because normal guys like us have been doing these styles of racing for over a century. I don't know about you though, but when my parents called me special, the reference wasn't that great. If you tell your friends you're going vintage racing when you're really heading to the go-kart track, you may have rode that short bus.

Family Cars

We recently had an opportunity to review the last 100 years of my families photos and I was surprised at the number of times my family has taken photos with cars as the subject or background. This got me thinking about the influence the cars in our families have.

Almost every day families interact with their car, and the car shares in memories like road-trip vacations and visits to the grandparents. Cars undoubtedly leave a lasting imprint on the character of a family, be it a family like mine, or a famous racing family, and if you look it's almost easy to see the automotive influence passed down.

In my family archives, most notable was Grandpa's 1957 Chevy, black on silver 2 door Bel-Air (the all American car). A beautiful quick car, yet practical with seating for a family of six with two bench seats. The car embodies an American dream of a successful middle-class family life.

My aunt sent me a note about the Bel Air, "I remember that old Bel Air, I spent many hours totally nauseated from car-sickness in the back of that thing! That's pretty much where I learned how to deal with car-sickness, and it's never happened to me since! But I also remember going on picnics, and we used to actually go on long Sunday drives out into the country, and passing tepees, which I thought was weird because they were on fire. Of course they were lumber mill tepees, a thing that I believe exists only in the past now. I remember looking up at the moon from the cavernous back seat and feeling so special because the moon was following me. Hey, I was 4 years old! And I don't remember ever wearing a seat belt. The entire back seat was my domain!"

The evidence in the photos tells me my family adopted automobiles fairly early in their development. By taking family photos with their cars it tells me that travel was important to my family and they connected to their cars as a useful and enjoyable tool that had earned a place in the family photos for services rendered. A tall order for any piece of equipment! Ever seen a family gathered around a washing machine?

The car my family chose was practical being tall to traverse ruts, and large enough to accommodate a family, but there was still a note of fun by choosing to go with a ragtop rather than a hardtop. And the dog made it into the pictures too!

As time passed, we succumbed to the need of a hardtop, and the family grew. If all of the relatives in the below picture traveled to the photo shoot in the vehicle pictured, my family may have been the clown posse of a travelling carnival.

Just how loved the family cars were shows when a forefather decided to catch a beautiful winter event in photograph by capturing the cars in the scene! And the cars, although newer, are still family oriented practical cars, slightly sporty.

What strikes me about our family vehicles is that the vehicles owned generations later are similar in traits. My parent's car growing up was a Chevy Blazer with a balanced and blueprinted motor. In shape and use, it shared much with cars from my family's past. Practical and family friendly with a slightly fun side. It made many hour trips to Costco (we lived in the country) with all four of us on board, but it could also tear across the desert, I learned when it became my vehicle.

My own family uses a Nissan Xterra. I would argue it is almost the exact vehicle in concept. Slightly sporty family hauler. So essentially my family has been buying the same vehicle for 100 years.

My family is not alone in this follow-the-leader game. You often hear of sons following their fathers into racing, or the racing being a family affair. I can imagine why this would happen. If growing up you thought of cars as something sporty to be driven fast, why wouldn't you choose to use cars in the way you've been taught? Racing is ripe with these stories, although unfortunately more than a few examples have ended in tragedy.

With no sense of organization other than the order in which I think of them, let's take a look at some of those famous family racing dynasties.

The famous F1 driver Graham Hill, pride of Great Britain and I believe the stereotype for more than one dashing cinema British villain is a prime example. Imagine growing up watching your father become the world champion racing the hottest cars of the time! What effect would that have on your life and how would you think of cars?

Well, in this particular example, Damon Hill became the first F1 world champion to follow his father to victory. Yet the family photos online show that he was immersed in the culture of racing cars from the youngest age. On the Getty Images website I came across a picture of a toddler Damon Hill in a pedal car surrounded by racing greats Stirling Moss, Graham Hill, Bruce McLaren, Wolfgang Von Trips and Jo Bonnier.

It wasn't always fathers that led the children into racing. Take for example the case of Pat Moss. Her brother, Stirling Moss, was on his way towards the top of motor racing. Pat had previously been involved in competitive horse events but surely her brother must have had some influence on her decision to go car racing. She starts rally racing and becomes the first woman to outright win an international rally. The family dinner conversations and weekend events must have had some influence on her desire and skills.

Replica of a Pat Moss rally car

Earlier today I saw a fun YouTube video of a short wheel base Ferrari 250GTO (https://www.youtube.com/watch?v=KHgD0wJGcR0) but before you watch race car driver Derek Hill push the most expensive car in the world around corners with a screaming V12, remember that his father is the famous American race car driver, Phil Hill, who drove the same Ferrari to victory in the 1960s at races like Sebring.

And let's face it, American racing has numerous examples of sons who followed their father successfully into racing. Earnhardt stickers decorate the rear bumper of every would-be NASCAR couch racer. Or consider the Petty racing generations. Richard Petty's number 43

Hemi is one of the best looking cars ever to drive in NASCAR, and one of the fastest; regulation having slowed cars since then.

Petty's son Kyle has over 500 Cup starts to his record. Sadly Kyle's son Adam, who also was following in the family footsteps, was lost in an accident.

And like the Earnhardt and Petty family, sadly tragedy has also often followed racing families through the generations.

Consider England's land speed record breaking father and son, Malcolm and Donald Campbell. Both pursued land and water top speed records until both lost their life in the pursuit, separated by some odd 30 years or so.

Or how about Italy's father and son racers Antonio and Alberto Ascari, both Grand Prix champions? From wikipedia – "There were several similarities between the deaths of Alberto and his father. Alberto Ascari died on 26 May 1955, at the age of 36. Antonio Ascari was also 36 when he died, on 26 July 1925 (Alberto was only four days older). Both were killed four days after surviving serious accidents and on the 26th day of the month. Both had crashed fatally at the exit of fast left-hand corners and both left behind a wife and two children."

Fortunately not all family racing legacies are marred by tragedy. Consider the Unser family. Beyond a father and son who both dominated racing at some point in their career, they've also shared an ability to move from Indy to NASCAR racing.

But we can't all be champion race car drivers and there are few fathers to lead sons in this direction. The list of F1, Grand Prix and Indy champions is probably less than

200 men long for all time. So what about the normal parents? Well, a fun search using photo sharing sites like Flickr is to look up "Family Car". You'll find many pictures of station wagons on road trips with smiling families gathered around.

The long and the short of it is, you were likely influenced by your parent's vehicles. Kids spend a lot of time in and around their parent's cars and the character of those cars is likely to have an effect on the kids.

So when you purchase your next vehicle consider that you'll be doing your family a favor by purchasing the more expensive 4x4 SUV if you use it for some notable adventures. Or, maybe you should buy that Hemi powered Challenger and take your son to a track day or two in it. Do you want them doomed to a life of boring vehicles because it's the model you set when you didn't want to spend a little extra for all-wheel-drive or some horsepower? Can you say the word Prius and adventure in the same sentence? I think not.

Track Day

I took the MGA out for its first track day and it was AWESOME! What a blast! And there was even an off-track excursion (more on that later). I thought I'd give a quick update even though I'm supposed to be building a crib right now... so I'll keep it short. That's best anyways, less of my poor grammar you have to read through.

But first, a quick side note. Seriously, they fired Jeremy Clarkson for punching someone for not doing their job?! That's not what you do with a politically incorrect guy like that! He'll just feel supremely vindicated. They should have made him wear a princess suit for an episode of Top Gear; act like a princess, be treated like a princess. That would have been more appropriate and might actually have affected his ego.

Back to the track - how'd this track day idea start? Well, about a month ago a friend mentioned the Autocross Club of Central Oregon was hosting a track day at the Oregon Raceway Park. He recommended I should attend. Dubious that a car as ugly a mine could pass a track tech inspection I didn't think much about it. Then two things happened: 1. my good friend Andrew encouraged me to go, and 2. Pete Brock (the designer of the 1960s Corvette Stingray and Daytona Shelby) wrote an article saying "Get out there and race."

I spent many nights in the garage tidying things up prepping. I even put some cheap rocker panels on that I bought off eBay years ago for $80 that don't fit very well. I figured missing body parts might be a reason to ban me from the track. I just bolted them on though, because they don't fit very well. Turns out metal rockers should cost more than $80. I did coat them with Rustoleum, so they shouldn't cause rust problems. Turns out, because I painted them dark blue, you could barely tell they were there anyways.

Getting the doors to adjust tight was also a total pain in the butt. Supposedly you should get the striker to click twice when closing the door. I could not make the driver's door click more than once so I eventually adjusted the door so that one click was tight! Oh, and side note. If you're rebuilding an MGA, you cannot get the doors to close tight without the rubber stops at the bottom; just bought two of those and they make a WORLD of difference! No more rattling over bumps (much); it makes the car SO much quieter to drive.

Still not believing it was ready to go to a track day three hours from town I went out for a three hour drive with my car group the weekend before. We had a great time driving around the hills and farmland West of Portland OR and the MGA kept up with a number of much newer cars all day without issue.

Finally it was track day! Now the Oregon Raceway Park (ORP) is three hours from Portland, and we were driving to ORP before dawn. The moon was awesome and only later did I find out it was the "blood moon" (earth gets between the sun and moon).

The track was gorgeous, out in the Central Oregon rolling grasslands. The track rolls in and out of the natural ridge lines of the area leading to excellent banked corners and blind corners leading to drop offs and "half-pipes".

Uh oh... busted. The wife just came home early from the baby shower and I haven't even started the crib...

Well... I survived.

So back to the story. The pits were a little intimidating. A few track only cars that looked pretty high speed (literally) were in attendance. My car looked a little out-of-place, but thankfully there were a few other ghetto cars in attendance (old Datsun 230, shell of a VW Rabbit).

The beginner class had some other small bore cars, many of them much faster than mine but not too intimidating, including the Rabbit. At first we had an instructor, but he eventually let me off on my own.

I was surprisingly calm. Autocross races will often get my adrenalin pumping but not so much this. Maybe it was because we weren't actually racing, or maybe it's because autocross is a short burst, but regardless, my instructor had to tell me they might flag me in if I kept my arm on the driver's window cause it looks like I'm not taking it serious enough. They obviously don't drive British cars because although my arm is on the window, my hand is on the wheel; there's just not much room in the cab!

The elevation changes were a blast! There's even a hairpin left that dives steeply off a hill to a long right corner! Great stuff! The skinny tires on the MGA were nearly squealing in every corner, and often were.

The "half-pipe", a heavily banked corner (like the name implies) was just awesome. The car'd pitch over like a boat on a large wave but it was fun. I went with the mid-size MGB sway-bar when building the front end but I might want to bump up to the bigger, earlier bar. I felt like I had to lean to counteract my sway!

Between each heat I'd look over the car and try and find loose intake bolts, lug nuts, etc. I couldn't find anything wrong with her. She never even got hot although often I was getting her up over 5000 RPMs (something I'd been terrified to do before this weekend because, hey,... I rebuilt the motor).

I think I'm putting on my sunglasses below but it looks like I'm trying to divine what might be going wrong. Camaraderie in the pits was great! Some very friendly people at the track on Track Day!

On the track I was surprised the stripped rabbit, with a Weber side-draft on each cylinder, decided to hang with me. I'm pretty sure his car is much faster but it was kind of flattering!

I went off the track twice. Once in a pretty slow corner with no-one around to see (not a flagged corner) with all four tires, but I bounced back on mostly in the same direction. A second time I just had too much speed and ended up under-steering two wheels into the grass.

But Andrew beat me in terms of off track excursions. His Go-Pro like system showed us he shifted right at the top of "Valkyrie Hill", which is a slight corner, causing his car to lose traction and send him spinning into the grass throwing up a 10 foot high wave of grass and dirt in front of him.

Unfortunately the grass rolled three of Andrew's tires beads back and deposited a large amount of dirt in them. We spent several hours cleaning those beads out with a tire iron and screw driver. In the below picture you can see the tire iron in the gravel while Andrew attempts to blow some of the dirt accumulated in the car out before his dusty drive home.

I was so proud of my track day prepping that I even took a picture of my wares, but ironically I forgot a valve stem removal tool which would have come in very handy.

My car did great all day but on the way home started making a weird buzzing sound at 2500 RPM. I stopped once to look but couldn't find anything. Once home I discovered the bolt and washer at the back of the alternator were loose and the washer was vibrating. I tried to tighten it but the hole stripped. I must have the alternator a little out of adjustment for that to happen... Or I stripped the hole when I put the alternator in but I don't remember that. I'll just get a self-threading bolt, the next size up. Should take care of it I hope.

But for the most part, the car did excellent, never even overheating, and I had a blast. This is what I want to use the MGA for, not car shows or driving to work. It didn't make me think autocross was boring though, I'm still going to do those too. They're different but still fun; I was wondering if I'd still think so after this weekend.

I'm thinking about not even fixing the MGA body much, and starting to put race parts in the car one by one (roll cage, fuel cell, etc.) because I had so much fun. A coat of flat Rustoleum may be the only paint job she gets, and as long as she does this well every weekend, I'll be a VERY happy camper. Track days are AWESOME! But so is autocross. And I'm going to try hill climbs this year. Long story short, using the MGA hard is awesome. I'd highly recommend it.

Go Racing!!!

Browsing through this month's Classic Motorsports magazine I read through Pete Brock's article, which essentially said, "Go racing." But Pete Brock is an engineer, and the article read a little like an engineer's blog, technical and wordy. I thought I'd try my hand at the same article, but in layman's terms for us simpler folks. What I'm really hoping to do is show you it doesn't matter what kind of hoopty car you have, you can get involved with competition and have a blast.

Pete Brock Designed This

First the personal testimony; for the last four years or so I've been trying all sorts of new motor sports. They are a complete kick in the pants. Some of them give you adrenalin rushes. Some of them make your technical skills better. Some of them give you great camaraderie with friends and other participants. I cannot recall once leaving an event and wishing I hadn't went, even when the rallycross filled my car with an inch of dirt.

What type of racing? Here are some suggestions and encouragement to "Just do it."

Got an old American car? Finally bought that Chevelle but couldn't afford the SS? Or maybe you're driving the slant six Dodge Swinger. It doesn't matter!! Go drag racing! There are fast and slow cars at drag races, and you're going to have fun. Some of the amateur classes are run so that you get different release times, for different cars. In other words, it tests your reaction time (green light, go) rather than your car; in these races you might beat a high performance SS 396 Camaro with your stock Vega! And you'll have fun!

Is your car a little sportier? In your free time do you enjoy carving corners? Take the car to an autocross. Yes, it seems silly driving around cones in a parking lot, but it actually is a complete rush. You're on a very tight track forcing you to have quick reactions and fine tire placement. It's quite a challenge, and I've left more than one autocross sprint with a slight adrenaline shake. And your car doesn't need to be amazing. I did it in a lethargic 1979 MGB. I've seen crossovers do it. You won't be the most ridiculous car there, and even if you are no one will care. I know, the MGA's door flew open and no one even mentioned it.

Not a speedy guy? Do you enjoy your car but would prefer a more "respectable" pace? Join a Time-Speed-Distance rally. Find a friend that's an engineer to do the math. In these "races" you're pushed to complete "sections" in exact times, rather than race through them. I've heard rumors of "open" sections, where it's as fast as you can go, but in my experience it's always under the speed limit. The challenges are: not getting lost, following directions, and getting your math right. As you do this you get a whole lot of car time to b.s. with your buddy and have fun. It's a great laid back atmosphere. Here in Portland these are on the first Friday night of every month and run around the country back roads for a couple hours; a great start to the weekend!

Are you a little grittier? Does your car have All-Wheel-Drive and you're not afraid to use it? Do you like to be sideways on a mountain road with a ribbon of dust following you? Try a rallycross. These are short courses, much like autocross except off road. In my experience, the courses are a little longer than autocross but it's very similar skills, except now you have dirt rather than asphalt for grip. If you don't think throwing your car sideways through a dust filled corner is fun, you might not be breathing. These are a complete blast. Just be aware, you may need your spare tire and if you see oil pressure drop shut-er-down NOW. It is possible to bust an oil pan on these outings. But who cares? You're having fun! You can fix oil pans and tire holes! Live a little!

Loving the pavement but autocross getting a little boring? Well, head for the track day! They let my hoopty MGA out on a track day, I'm sure they'll let your car out (as long as it's mechanically sound, and if it's a convertible it must have a roll bar). This allows you to experience corners as fast as you care to take them without worrying about Johnny Law! Everyone is going the same direction too. No drunken F250 drivers heading down your side of the highway on a public mountain road! Mostly, the only person that can mess you up is yourself! You'll have a great time, and you'll get to know other guys with a similar passion as you. Give it a try! I'll bet money you enjoy it. And it doesn't matter much what you drive.

You might even drive off the track. A lot of tracks have runoffs. They're designed to let you go sliding. Take, for example, an excursion by my buddy. No big deal. Some dirt in the tire beads were the only issue after it was done. We spent a couple hour cleaning the dirt out from around the bead so the tires would hold air again and he was good to drive home.

I don't own the picture but you can see it here - http://www.sublightphotography.com/accotrackday/i0 eoyxza7hmxfeayr7okh150esrvcq

Did you build a car with a lot of torque and great suspension? Give hillclimbs a try! I'm sorry to say I haven't done this yet, but I have every intention of trying this year. We have several here locally and I'd bet you do too. I've been watching videos of them on YouTube and they look like a blast. Probably the closest things you could get to a closed road race in this modern US of bubble babies, warning signs, and security blankets. Have fun! Point the nose to the sky and see how much guts you have going around those corners with steep drop offs! And if you go slow, who knows or cares? You don't even have to tell your buddies you went, and even if you do they probably have no context and won't know or care if you drive like your grandmothers poodle.

These are all cheap, fun ways for the average guy to get out competing! Give them a try! You might find you enjoy them. That's when the trouble starts if you ask me. Now I'm researching what it would cost to make my car Vintage Racing Series legal. Fuel cells, roll bars, harnesses, etc. The prices start to add up very fast. But it'll be fun and worth it, and I learned that from doing the events above. Find out for yourself. Wear that proud smile of "I did it!" And I repeat, it doesn't matter what you drive. I did it with a beat up old MGB and MGA. Very beat up.

Just Say No To Wild Hairs

Ok, I apologize in advance for giving you an "update" about painting a classic car that's going to turn out to be mostly pictures with a few snarky comments. Between trying to get a car painted, 12 hour shifts at work, a side business (collectiblebooks.org), a young family (two below two) and occasionally friends... I have NO time. Last night I accidentally passed out at 9 although I was planning on staying awake until 1 a.m. posting books to the book business; my body said, "You're done."

Anyways, I have no stinking idea why but one day I got tired of looking at the holes in the bottom of the MGA's body. I was done with them. Over it. I wanted them fixed. So I yanked the fenders off and started fixing them myself. I couldn't afford repair parts but the fab shop sold me a long, 2' wide piece of 18 gauge for $15, and that I could afford. So I figured I'd learn to panel beat. I'd bought a cheap set of Harbor Freight bodywork hammers some time ago, so why not?

I cut metal pieces to fit and used the hammer and dolly's to shape them. Turns out the long C shaped dolly in the Harbor Freight body set has a similar contour to body shapes. I could just bang the pieces along that dolly and they would eventually get pretty close.

Filling all the holes took forever. The difficulty was compounded by my $10 welding helmet that did not have the auto-darkening feature. Combination of guess work and following the glowing orange blob allowed me to eventually fill the holes.

And I was done with the welding by braille. I went down to HF (Harbor Freight) on Father's Day and bought an auto-darkening helmet after the 1st fender. Because it was father's day, and I had a coupon, I left with the helmet for $55 or so. SOOOOO WORTH IT!!! More on that later. Also, I was given a free LED light.

My second panel was in better shape so I didn't have as much to do. Also, I was getting better with the dollys and I was getting prouder of the results. And the auto-darkening helmet allowed me to see where I was putting the gun before I pulled the trigger. Awesome. I should have bought that helmet years ago.

By the third panel I was done with filling little holes. I replaced most of the bottom of it in one shot.

After a lot of welding and grinding it came out in pretty good shape. It'll definitely be 20-20 awesome (at 20 feet and 20 M.P.H. it will look great)!

The fourth fender I was very scared of. It had several different body lines that were completely missing.

But, with three fenders under my belt I got to pounding on the dollys and cutting.

I was quite proud of the end result.

Now here's what I don't get. Originally I thought, well, let's just primer those up and keep on driving it. Somehow I went from that, to "Let's strip this beast". I'm not quite sure how that happened.

My wife did express a desire to do more things as a family and blamed the car for some of our time "not together". Since we have two kids, the MGA has become a "Daddy's going for a drive car" because I can't take them. We're thinking of selling the MGA and finding something with four seats. I think that might have weighed in on my decision to strip it, thinking if it was one color it'd be easier to sell.

I was thinking flat black with some pinstriping. Sound cheesy? Well, Von Dutch pinstriped an MGA so I think that makes it a period look! And for those of you wondering, "Wait, Von Dutch didn't just design my hat?",... I bet the Southern California weather is nice you lucky spoiled rich kids.

But it turns out this is a LOT of work. Two days with a power sander to strip the bulk, with a 3rd day of hand sanding with even finer grit sandpaper.

Which got me thinking... Is all this worth it for flat black? Would I ever want to do this again? Should I just paint it nice?

Well, that line of thinking presented some problems. A, my panel gap wasn't very nice. It turns out the $60 (with shipping) rocker panels (under the door) did not fit very well.

So then I thought, "No problem, those British car magazines guys fix their cars with hammers. I have hammers, I'll fix all the dents with my welder/grinder/hammers! I don't even need Bondo."

Why do I hate Bondo? Well, I've never had the patience to wait for it to dry, I've never got the edges to disappear, and I'm always left with crater size holes you could drive the rover moon vehicle through.

Of course when I was drilling the holes to mount the new steel to the MGA, the cheap Harbor Freight drill-bit snapped sending the broken fragment of a drill bit spinning into my hand with the full pushing weight of my arm behind it at 1000 RPM. Nice little hole out of that one. I think my wife's gotten used to me holding appendages coming in from the garage saying "Where are the *$#@ bandages?!" We didn't have any bandages today so I used a paper towel and masking tape (couldn't find my Duck Tape either).

In the end though, I got everything to fit pretty well.

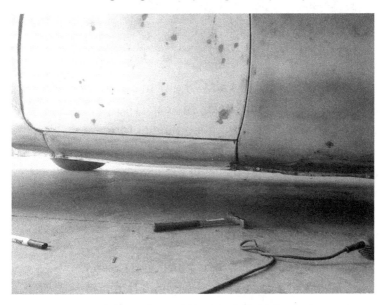

Oh, and a side note, LED lights are AWESOME, especially for welding. With any other type of light, if the welding material drips on it you get an explosion and your light is done. With the LEDs... no explosion, no drama, etc. You lose the tiny bulb that gets the direct contact but the rest keep on trucking. LEDs rock in the garage.

My anti-rust coating has arrived and when I'm done fitting the driver's side I'll get that on the car. The days/months to do the car right are looming before me and I'm very afraid I just don't have the time. I'm starting to, gasp, consider flat blacking the car again. Maybe I won't even do Bondo, that way when I go to sell the car I can just tell whoever is buying it that there is no Bondo and what they see it what they get.

But if I do that the car is not worth as much and I won't be able to get as fun of a car to jam the whole family in for Cars'n'Coffee or a trip to the coast/mountain (I'd drastically prefer the mountain to the rainy, windy area the people in Oregon call a coast; living in Hawaii ruined my appreciation of Oregon beaches).

Decisions, decisions. Wait, I have to go. The little one's nap time is over. Probably flat black.

Lime Rock Historic Festival

Sunday morning I found myself at the best car show I've ever attended, with almost unlimited access to many cars I've only seen in sports car magazines and news articles about record setting sales results. The Lime Rock Historic Festival in Connecticut left me astounded at the vehicles I could walk up to and drool over without anyone once saying, "Sir, please step away from the car".

715

1968 Lamborghini
Miura

We even asked a number of people to open hoods and doors with only the friendliest of responses. Maybe Prozac is distributed in the water supply in this friendly, historic and picturesque state. It was almost as though the owners were saying, "You're finished drooling on my paintwork and would now like to drool on my interior? I'd be happy to open the door to my million dollar car to find a home for your spittle".

The highlights of the show for me were the Mercedes factory racing cars. I've read legends, watched documentaries, etc., about the Silver Arrows. Finally at Lime Rock I was able to see the legend in person.

The Silver Arrow cars are the stuff of folklore. Here was a car designed to prove world dominance in a hugely unstable political climate where such a feat was almost possible. A book could easily be filled with the context, politics, races, technologies, drivers and etc. associated with the Silver Arrows.

The onsite curator told me the 1939 W154 car guzzles a gallon of gas like fluid a mile. Inside the cockpit there is a suspension adjustment control because the car changes weight drastically as the 90+ gallon gas tank drains, requiring multiple suspension settings between fuel stops.

I'm sad to report that I didn't get a good photo of Juan Fangio's 1955 car although it's a car and driver I've loved watching race (and dominate) in vintage films.

Moving on, I will say Ralph Lauren's black Mercedes is stunning.

A 1908 Mercedes "Brooklands" race car was a testament to the nature of Brooklands racing. Beastly in proportions, chain driven with little to no suspension technology or protection for the driver, this car is an artifact of one of the most dangerous and brave times in racing history.

On the more personal side, one of the people interaction highlights at the show was chatting with the 1950s NASCAR racer Russ Truelove, who still owns and drives his race car which lived through two race seasons, including a nasty flip at Daytona.

One of the best looking cars I came across was a beautiful blue Maserati.

There were a number of rarities I'd not seen before, one of which Russian and the other I still know nothing about.

Two Stutz rally cars added to my tally of cars I'd never seen in person before.

And having never seen a Bristol before, I was surprised
to walk up on a group of 5 of them. Powered by a triple
downdraft carb system on a straight six, they're likely to
peppy and they are great looking cars.

In the pits I found several 1950s era race cars that
looked like something straight out of a Speed Racer
cartoon.

There was also a stunning Speed Racer out along the track.

And then an Allard revolted against all the race car beauty providing an excellent example of function before form. What a beast! Check out those Hemi heads on a 1940s American V8.

Italian beauties were everywhere. I wouldn't be surprised if you added up every vintage Italian beauty I've seen in my life and the number was smaller than the number of Italian gems I saw today.

The British Empire cars were out in their own force.

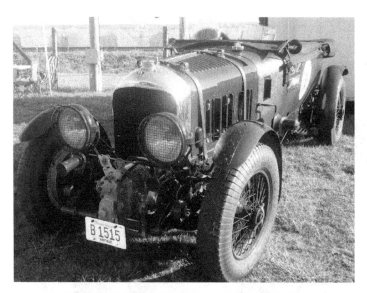

As were the Germans!

Including this Mercedes 300 with every doo-dad available for a 300 SL including the shaving kit, luggage, and spare fuses box.

I enjoyed perusing the Pre-WWII Great Gatsby cars.

The new class for un-restored vehicles brought in some fun entries. Probably difficult as hell to judge, but fun to look at!

And some very nice vintage, historic motorcycles could be found throughout the event.

And, although oddities, the last two cars I'll share pictures of sit very highly on the list of cars I'd like to drive hard.

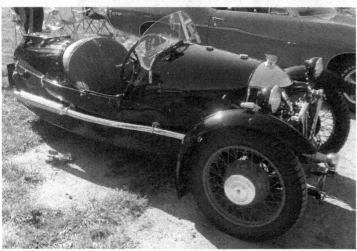

The MGA Sold, Some Final Thoughts

Well, it finally happened, someone bought the MGA! They had a caveat though, I had to put it back together, without paint, so they could drive it immediately to car shows. This caused a week of hectic work! But, it's behind me now and I have a little time to reflect on the car.

Before the buyer arrived for their first look at the car, I knew I had to get the body lines to match up better. The rockers I bought arrived too small (as is typical of many repair parts these days). I had to weld extension pieces onto the rockers and then adjust the fenders accordingly. Because the doors were functioning (moderately) well, I never removed them. Door alignments scare me and I'll do just about anything to avoid them.

About the hour I got the rockers lined up the buyer came to review the car. She loved it. She has a project coupe at home but wanted something that she could drive "now".

The woman decided she wanted the MGA as long as I'd put all the parts back on. She offered to provide a down-payment so I could take it off Craigslist. I told her there was no need, I trusted her, and I'd take payment in-full at delivery. As I put the car back together I started getting real scared because I realized she had no incentive to come back!

Once back together the MGA looked fantastic, like a WWII aluminum skinned fighter plane. I heard rumor that there's a chemical you can put on bare metal to keep it from rusting. If the buyer hadn't returned I'd have tried to find that and keep the bare metal look. Maybe the buyer will do just that.

Thankfully the buyer did come back. It was a little bitter-sweet. She drove away in a nicer car then I'd ever had. I don't have the receipts (I gave them to her) but I'm relatively sure I spent at least as much as she paid ($10.5k) although I was keeping track and it was pretty close. She basically got 3 years of free labor!

Yes, 3 years. That's how long I worked on the MGA. It was what is known as a rolling-restoration; I'd fix one thing and put it back on the road for another event (autocross, track day, etc.). I had a blast in the car and loved it.

Why did I sell the MGA? Well, mainly because as my family expanded (two kids) the MGA became a loner activity. Now those can be good, but I already own a dual-sport motorcycle. I want to bring my family to an occasional Cars 'n Coffee, or drive them to the coast on the weekend. Those things just aren't as fun by yourself.

What can I say about the MGA? Well, if you're just getting into car restoration I don't think there's a simpler car out there with more parts availability. Seriously, if you get stuck on something you just jump on the forum and someone will answer your question within an hour (at most). It's insane. You can buy every part and the associated MGA culture is very accepting and helpful.

And it's fun! Throwing it through a dirt rallycross race and driving it at an ORP track day are two of my ownership highlights! The MGA is a great car, well balanced, that clearly communicates its limits, has excellent steering feel, and sits so low you feel like you're speeding when you're actually being a law abiding citizen. It's great.

But it's not a family car.

So what's next for me?

Well, I realized you can buy an early 2000's BMW M3 for just a little more than I sold the MGA for. It fits four, has 330 h.p., rear wheel drive, and paddle shifters. I can't find anything comparable at the price (except for a Mustang, but I'm sorry to say that I feel like I need to be from Mexico to drive one with their gaudy stripes and etc.). I'm in discussions to purchase the BMW below. I once owned a similar year 3 series that was a complete dog. In the one month of ownership it had $600 dollars in parts break. I'm really hoping that it's true that the M3 is built at a different plant, one where the workers aren't all stoned and missing their opposable thumbs (I can't figure out how else they built such an awful car as my last BMW).

I'll miss the MGA, but I won't miss living in the garage. With my growing family and side book business (CollectibleBooks.org), I just don't have time. Maybe there's another MGA in my future, 20 years from now. Just about when I've forgotten everything probably.

To those of you that followed my time with the MGA, thanks for coming along for the journey! I hope you enjoyed reading about my escapades. Maybe there'll be BMW stories... but I doubt it because people with popped collars would read that kind of blog and I just don't relate. I'm going to be the offbeat dirty t-shirt wearing M3 owner all the other M3 owners try to pretend doesn't exist or I might bring down the value of their cars.